U0085023

序 言

　　十二年國民基本教育即將施行，考試型態也因此隨之改變。根據教育部公布的最新施測方法，「國中基本學力測驗」，將被「國中教育會考」所取代。相較於以往的國中基測，兩者最大的差異是，國中教育會考加入「**英語聽力測驗**」，目標是希望讓英文更貼近日常生活的使用，並修正以往只注重英語閱讀能力的考試方式。

　　要在「聽力測驗」得高分，就是要不斷地練習，培養出語感，平時聽 MP3 練習時，**一定要養成「先看選項，再聽題目」**的習慣。看選項的速度一定要超前，如果哪一道題目聽不懂，就必須放棄，立刻看下一題的選項，這樣才能掌握答題的重點，及縮短做答的時間。千萬不要等聽完題目，再看選項，否則整個聽力考試，都會失敗。

　　「**國中會考英語聽力測驗①**」共十二回，每回有三十題。每回分別依照教育部公布之範例，分成三部分：辨識句意、基本問答、言談理解。題目皆是生活常用情景及對話。做完這十二回，必能熟悉國中教育會考英語科聽力測驗模式，一舉獲得高分。

　　書中有些美國的習慣口語，特別在背景說明中詳加解釋，一般中國人不會的慣用語，就是勝過別人的關鍵。在編審及校對的每一階段，均力求完善，但恐有疏漏之處，誠盼各界先進不吝批評指正。

編者 謹識

國中教育會考英語科聽力測驗說明

一、評量理由

　　國民中小學九年一貫課程綱要明訂英語科課程同時注重聽、說、讀、寫的教學，而國中基測英語科自施行以來，僅評量學生閱讀能力，考試結果僅能說明學生局部的英語能力。就測驗評量專業角度而言，尚有效度表徵不足之慮，若國中教育會考配合課程綱要內涵，針對國中生英語聽力進行綜合評量，將有助於提升測驗評量效度，亦對國中英語教育產生正面影響。

二、測驗方式、題本架構及示例

(一) 測驗方式

1. 英語聽力＋英語閱讀，總共 60-75 題，其中聽力部分 20-30 題，閱讀部分 40-45 題，合併實施進行。
2. 測驗時間共 80 分鐘，先進行聽力測驗 20 分鐘，再進行閱讀測驗 60 分鐘。
3. 聽力測驗均為三選一的單選題，目前僅先規劃單題。

(二) 題本架構

	題型	測驗內容（評量目標）	題數分配
聽力 （20-30題） （三選一）	單題	辨識句意（單句+圖表）	3-10
		基本問答（單一對話）	7-10
		言談理解 （短文及對話，評量細節、推論、猜字、主旨等）	10
聽力測驗每題均播音兩次，兩次播音之間停頓 5 秒。			
閱讀 （40-45題） （四選一）	單題	語言基礎成分 （字彙/語意+語法）	12-20
	題組	篇章理解 （克漏字+整段式）	25-35
聽力＋閱讀：60-75 題			

(三) 示例

1. 評量目標：辨識句意

> （錄音稿）John enjoys taking a bath.

選出符合句子描述的圖片。

(A)　　　　　　　　(B)　　　　　　　　(C)*

2. 評量目標：基本問答

> （錄音稿）Hi, Mike. I haven't seen you for a long time.
> How are you doing?

選出最適合的回答，完成對話。

(A) I'm watching TV.

(B) I'm OK, thanks.*

(C) I'm at school.

3. 評量目標：言談理解（推論）

> （錄音稿）
> （男聲）May I help you?
> （女聲）Yes, I'd like to look at that red sweater. How much is it?
> （男聲）It's one thousand dollars.

Question: Where are the man and the woman?

(A) In a restaurant.

(B) In the living room.

(C) In a department store.*

4. 評量目標：言談理解（猜字）

（錄音稿）
（男聲）Did you read *Girls' Talk*?
（女聲）Yes, and I liked it. It helps me a lot. You should also read it.
（男聲）Mm… I'll go buy it right away.

Question: What's *Girls' Talk*?
(A) A movie.
(B) A computer game.
(C) A book.*

國中會考英文聽力 ①

一、辨識句意

本部分共 10 題，每題有三個圖片選項，請聽光碟放音機播出的題目，聽後從試題冊上 A、B、C 圖片中，選出一個最適合的回答。每題播出二遍。

例： （聽） John enjoys taking a bath.
　　 （看）

(A)　　　　　　　　(B)　　　　　　　　(C)

正確答案為 C，請在答案紙上塗黑作答。

1.　　　A.　　　　　　　B.　　　　　　　C.

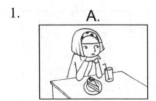  

2.　　　A.　　　　　　　B.　　　　　　　C.

 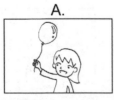 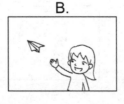 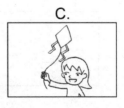

3.

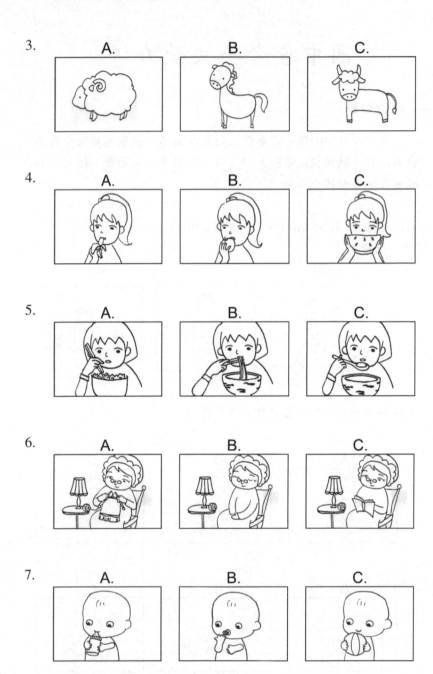

8.

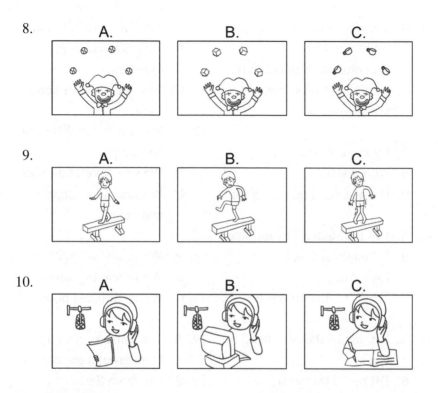

9.

10.

二、基本問答：選出最適合的回答，完成對話。

本部份共 10 題，每題光碟放音機會播出一個問句或直述句，聽後從試題冊上 A、B、C 三個選項中，選出一個最適合的回答。每題播出二遍。

例： （聽）Hi, Mike. I haven't seen you for a long time.
How are you doing?

（看）A. I'm watching TV.
B. I'm OK, thanks.
C. I'm at school.

正確答案為 B，請在答案紙上塗黑作答。

11. A. Thanks. I bought it at the night market.
　　B. Sometimes. I'm not sure.
　　C. Never. It looks great on you.

12. A. I was at school.
　　B. About sixty.
　　C. It was OK. I learned a lot.

13. A. I'm not such a fast thinker.
　　B. I thought it was interesting.
　　C. I didn't know about it.

14. A. No, his birthday is next week.
　　B. I'll be 15 this year.
　　C. They don't celebrate birthdays in my culture.

15. A. I'm always in a good mood.
　　B. My cat died yesterday.
　　C. Whenever I can.

16. A. Yes, I live in Taiwan.
　　B. Yes, it's been a great experience.
　　C. Yes, they love it here.

17. A. We saw many different paintings.
　　B. We saw several movies.
　　C. We saw lions, snakes, and bears.

18. A. We're almost there.
　　B. We're leaving soon.
　　C. We're finished now.

19. A. The noise is coming from around the corner.
　　B. I'm from Seoul.
　　C. I took the bus.

20. A. The banjo was a gift from my father.
　　B. Sure, I can play.
　　C. No. Now I'm learning to play piano.

三、言談理解（推論）

　　本部份共 10 題，每題光碟放音機會播出一段對話及一個相關的問題，聽後從試題冊上 A、B、C 三個選項中，選出一個最適合的回答。每題播出二遍。

例： （聽） (Man)　　May I help you?

　　　　　　 (Woman)　Yes, I'd like to look at that red sweater. How much is it?

　　　　　　 (Man)　　It's one thousand dollars.

　　　　　 Question:　Where are the man and the woman?

（看）　A. In a restaurant.

　　　　B. In the living room.

　　　　C. In a department store.

正確答案為 C，請在答案紙上塗黑作答。

21. A. In a restaurant.
　　B. In a library.
　　C. In a department store.

22. A. A book.
　　B. A television show.
　　C. A movie.

23. A. Classmates.
　　B. Co-workers.
　　C. Business partners.

24. A. Attending a party.
　　B. Having a party.
　　C. Babysitting.

25. A. At a street corner.
　　B. In an art museum.
　　C. On an airplane.

26. A. Robert is in trouble.
　　B. Robert is missing.
　　C. Robert is busy studying.

27. A. A small pizza with black olives and onion.
　　B. A medium pizza with ham and pineapple.
　　C. A large pizza with cheese and pepperoni.

28. A. Excited.
　　B. Nervous.
　　C. Indifferent.

29. A. On Saturday.
　　B. On Sunday.
　　C. On Monday.

30. A. She won a bet.
　　B. She won a contest.
　　C. She won the lottery.

國中會考英文聽力 ① 詳解

一、辨識句意

1. (**B**) Laura ordered a hamburger with fries.

   蘿拉點了一個漢堡跟薯條。

   * order〔'ɔrdɚ〕v. 點（菜）　　hamburger〔'hæmbɝgɚ〕n. 漢堡
   fries〔fraɪz〕n. pl. 薯條（= French fries）

2. (**C**) Larry is flying a kite. 賴瑞正在放風箏。

   * kite〔kaɪt〕n. 風箏　　***fly a kite*** 放風箏

3. (**B**) I went to the zoo and saw a horse. 我去動物園看到一匹馬。

   * zoo〔zu〕n. 動物園　　horse〔hɔrs〕n. 馬

4. (**A**) Becky enjoys eating bananas. 貝琪喜歡吃香蕉。

   * enjoy〔ɪn'dʒɔɪ〕v. 喜歡；享受　　***enjoy + V-ing*** 喜歡～
   banana〔bə'nænə〕n. 香蕉

5. (**B**) Sarah prefers noodles. 莎拉比較喜歡吃麵。

   * prefer〔prɪ'fɝ〕v. 比較喜歡　　noodle〔'nudl̩〕n. 麵（條）

6. (**C**) Grandma likes reading. 奶奶喜歡閱讀。

   * grandma〔'grændma〕n. 祖母；奶奶（= grandmother）
   read〔rid〕v. 閱讀

7. (**C**) The baby has a ball. 嬰兒有一顆球。

   * baby〔'bebɪ〕n. 嬰兒；小寶寶　　ball〔bɔl〕n. 球

8. (**C**) The clown is juggling teacups. 小丑用茶杯在耍把戲。

   * clown〔klaʊn〕n. 小丑
   juggle〔'dʒʌgl̩〕v. 耍（球、刀、盤子等）
   teacup〔'ti,kʌp〕n. 茶杯

9. (**A**) Jack has good balance. 傑克平衡感很好。

   * balance〔'bæləns〕*n.* 平衡

10. (**B**) Jane enjoys making music on her computer.
    珍喜歡在她電腦上製作音樂。

    * music〔'mjuzɪk〕*n.* 音樂
      computer〔kəm'pjutɚ〕*n.* 電腦

二、基本問答

11. (**A**) Where did you get that coat? It's really nice.
    你在哪裡買到那件大衣？真的很好看。

    A. Thanks. I bought it at the night market.
       謝謝。我在夜市買的。
    B. Sometimes. I'm not sure. 有時候。我不確定。
    C. Never. It looks great on you.
       從來沒有。穿在你身上很好看。

    * coat〔kot〕*n.* 大衣　　***night market*** 夜市
      sure〔ʃur〕*adj.* 確定的　　***look great on sb.*** 適合（某人）

12. (**C**) There you are, Bill. How was school today?
    比爾，總算看到你了。今天學校如何？

    A. I was at school. 我在學校。
    B. About sixty. 大約六十。
    C. It was OK. I learned a lot. 很好。我學到很多。

    * ***There you are.*** 你終於來了。【用於等待某人】
      learn〔lɜn〕*v.* 學習　　***a lot*** 很多

13. (**B**) Did you read the book I gave you? What did you think?
    你讀了我給你的書了嗎？你覺得如何？

    A. I'm not such a fast thinker. 我腦筋沒動這麼快。

B. I thought it was interesting. 我覺得很有趣。

C. I didn't know about it. 我不知道這件事情。

* *fast thinker* 思考敏捷的人
   interesting (ˈɪntərɪstɪŋ) *adj.* 有趣的

14. (**A**) Here comes Paul. Isn't it his birthday today?
   保羅來了。今天不是他的生日嗎？

   A. No, his birthday is next week. 不，他的生日在下週。

   B. I'll be 15 this year. 我今年要 15 歲了。

   C. They don't celebrate birthdays in my culture.
      在我們文化裡是不慶生的。

   * birthday (ˈbɝθ,de) *n.* 生日   celebrate (ˈsɛlə,bret) *v.* 慶祝
      culture (ˈkʌltʃɚ) *n.* 文化

15. (**B**) What's wrong? You seem really unhappy today.
   你怎麼了？你今天看起來很不高興。

   A. I'm always in a good mood. 我心情總是很好。

   B. My cat died yesterday. 我的貓昨天死了。

   C. Whenever I can. 隨時都可以。

   * *What's wrong?* 你（妳）怎麼了？   seem (sim) *v.* 看似
      unhappy (ʌnˈhæpɪ) *adj.* 不高興的   mood (mud) *n.* 心情
      in a good mood 心情好
      whenever (hwɛnˈɛvɚ) *conj.* 每當；隨時

16. (**B**) Wow, you've lived in Taiwan for six years! You must
   really like it here.
   哇，你已經住在台灣六年了！你一定很喜歡這裡。

   A. Yes, I live in Taiwan. 是的，我住在台灣。

   B. Yes, it's been a great experience.
      是的，這是個很棒的經驗。

   C. Yes, they love it here. 是的，他們很喜歡這裡。

   * *like it here* 喜歡這裡   experience (ɪksˈpɪrɪəns) *n.* 經驗

17. (**C**) So today was your class trip to the zoo. What did you see?

所以今天你們去動物園班遊，那你們看到什麼？

A. We saw many different paintings.

我們看到很多不同的畫。

B. We saw several movies. 我們看了好幾部電影。

C. We saw lions, snakes, and bears.

我們看到獅子、蛇和熊。

* ***class trip*** 班遊　　different〔ˈdɪfərənt〕*adj.* 不同的

painting〔ˈpentɪŋ〕*n.* 畫

several〔ˈsɛvərəl〕*adj.* 數個的　　lion〔ˈlaɪən〕*n.* 獅子

snake〔snek〕*n.* 蛇　　bear〔bɛr〕*n.* 熊

18. (**A**) We've been walking for an hour. Is it much further?

我們已經走了一個小時了，還很遠嗎？

A. We're almost there. 我們快到了。

B. We're leaving soon. 我們快離開了。

C. We're finished now. 我們做完了。

* further〔ˈfɝðɚ〕*adj.* 較遠的；更遠的

finished〔ˈfɪnɪʃt〕*adj.* 完成的；做完的

19. (**B**) I've never seen you around here before. Where are you from?

我之前在這沒看過你，你是來自哪裡？

A. The noise is coming from around the corner.

噪音是來自角落附近。

B. I'm from Seoul. 我來自首爾。

C. I took the bus. 我搭巴士。

* noise〔nɔɪz〕*n.* 噪音　　corner〔ˈkɔrnɚ〕*n.* 角落

Seoul〔sol〕*n.* 首爾【韓國（Korea）首都】

20. (**C**) Are you still taking violin lessons? 你還在上小提琴課嗎？

  A. The banjo was a gift from my father.

   這班究琴是我爸爸送的禮物。

  B. Sure, I can play. 當然，我會彈奏。

  C. No. Now I'm learning to play piano.

   <u>不，現在我開始學彈鋼琴了。</u>

  * violin〔͵vaɪə'lɪn〕*n.* 小提琴

   banjo〔'bændʒo〕*n.* 班究琴；五弦琴【用手指撥彈的一種弦樂器】

   take lessons 上課 gift〔gɪft〕*n.* 禮物

   piano〔pɪ'æno〕*n.* 鋼琴

   play piano 彈鋼琴【現代美語常省略 the】

三、言談理解

21. (**C**) M：How do the shoes fit?

  男：這鞋子合腳嗎？

  W：They're squeezing my toes a little bit.

  女：我的腳趾有一點被擠壓到。

  M：Let me see if we have a larger size in stock.

  男：我看看比較大的尺碼有沒有存貨。

  Question：Where does this conversation take place?

     這對話是在哪裡發生的？

  A. In a restaurant. 在餐廳。

  B. In a library. 在圖書館。

  C. In a department store. <u>在百貨公司。</u>

  * shoe〔ʃu〕*n.* 鞋子 fit〔fɪt〕*v.*（衣服等）適合

   squeeze〔skwiz〕*v.* 擠；壓 toe〔to〕*n.* 腳趾

   a little bit 有點 ***in stock*** 有存貨

   conversation〔͵kɑnvɚ'seʃən〕*n.* 對話

   take place 發生 restaurant〔'rɛstərənt〕*n.* 餐廳

   library〔'laɪ͵brɛrɪ〕*n.* 圖書館 ***department store*** 百貨公司

22. (**B**) M：Did you see *America's Top Model* last night?

男：妳昨晚有看「美國超級名模」嗎？

W：Yes, I did.　It was a very entertaining episode.

女：有呀，是很好看的一集。

M：I know.　I can't wait to see it next week.

男：我也這麼覺得，我等不及要看下週那集。

Question：What is *America's Top Model*?

　　　　「美國超級名模」是什麼？

A. A book. 一本書。

B. A television show. 電視節目。

C. A movie.　一部電影。

* top〔tɑp〕*adj.* 最佳的；最好的　　　model〔'mɑdl〕*n.* 模特兒
  entertaining〔͵ɛntə'tenɪŋ〕*adj.* 令人愉快的；有趣的
  episode〔'ɛpə͵sod〕*n.* (連續劇等) 一集
  can't wait to + V. 等不及要～
  show〔ʃo〕*n.* 表演；節目

23. (**A**) W：I failed the science exam today.

女：我今天的科學考試不及格。

M：Really?　I thought it was so easy!　What happened?
　　Didn't you study?

男：真的嗎？我覺得很簡單耶！發生什麼事了？妳沒唸書嗎？

W：I studied all week, except I studied the wrong chapters.

女：我整週都在唸書，但是我讀錯章節了。

Question：What is the relationship between the speakers?

　　　　這兩個說話者是什麼關係？

A. Classmates. 同班同學。

B. Co-workers.　同事。

C. Business partners.　商業夥伴。

* fail〔fel〕v. 考不及格　　science〔'saɪəns〕n. 科學
except〔ɪk'sɛpt〕conj. 除了；只是；但是（= except that）
chapter〔'tʃæptɚ〕n. 章節　　relationship〔rɪ'leʃən,ʃɪp〕n. 關係
speaker〔'spikɚ〕n. 說話者　　co-worker〔'ko,wɝkɚ〕n. 同事
partner〔'pɑrtnɚ〕n. 夥伴

24. (**C**) M：Hi, Polly. I'm having a party this Friday and I'd like
　　　　　　 you to come.

　　　男：嗨，波麗，我週五要辦個派對，我希望妳能來。

　　　W：Thanks, Jim. I wish I could, but I'm babysitting my
　　　　　 nephew on Friday.

　　　女：吉姆，謝謝你。我希望我能去，但是週五我得當保姆
　　　　　照顧我姪子。

　　　M：That's too bad. Maybe next time.

　　　男：真可惜。或許下次吧。

　　　Question：What is Polly doing this Friday?

　　　　　　　　波麗週五要做什麼？

　　　A. Attending a party. 參加派對。

　　　B. Having a party. 舉辦派對。

　　　C. Babysitting. 當保姆。

　　　* ***have a party***　舉辦派對
　　　　babysit〔'bebɪ,sɪt〕v. 擔任…的臨時保姆
　　　　nephew〔'nɛfju〕n. 姪子　　***That's too bad***. 真可惜。
　　　　attend〔ə'tɛnd〕v. 參加；出席

25. (**A**) W：Excuse me, sir. I'm new to the city. Could you please
　　　　　　　 help me?

　　　女：對不起，先生。我剛到這城市，可以請你幫幫我嗎？

　　　M：You do look a little lost. Where are you trying to go?

　　　男：妳的確看起來有點像是迷路了，妳想要去哪裡？

W：I'd like to visit the Museum of Modern Art.

女：我想去當代藝術博物館。

Question：Where is this conversation most likely taking place? 這對話最可能發生在哪裡？

A. At a street corner. 在街角。

B. In an art museum. 在藝術博物館。

C. On an airplane. 在飛機上。

Excuse me. 對不起。【用於引起對方注意力】

new〔nu〕*adj.* 剛來的；不熟悉的

do + *V.* 的確～；真的～

look〔lʊk〕*v.* 看起來　　lost〔lɔst〕*adj.* 迷路的

museum〔mju'ziəm〕*n.* 博物館

modern〔'madən〕*adj.* 現代的　　art〔art〕*n.* 藝術

likely〔'laɪklɪ〕*adj.* 可能的　　*take place* 發生

corner〔'kɔrnə〕*n.* 轉角　　airplane〔'ɛr,plen〕*n.* 飛機

26. (**C**) M：Have you seen Robert lately? I haven't seen him for a couple of weeks.

男：妳最近有沒有看到羅伯特？我有幾週沒看到他了。

W：Me neither. I hope he's OK.

女：我也是，我希望他沒什麼事。

M：I'm sure he's fine. Knowing Robert, I'll bet he's been studying for the final exam.

男：我確定他很好，就我對他的了解，我敢打賭他一直在為期末考唸書。

Question：What does the man think? 男子有什麼想法？

A. Robert is in trouble. 羅伯特有麻煩了。

B. Robert is missing. 羅伯特失蹤了。

C. Robert is busy studying. 羅伯特忙著唸書。

* lately〔'letlɪ〕*adv.* 最近（＝ *recently* ）
a couple of 幾個　　neither〔'niðɚ〕*adv.* 也（不）
sure〔ʃur〕*adj.* 確定的　　bet〔bɛt〕*v.* 打賭
final exam 期末考　　**in trouble** 有麻煩
missing〔'mɪsɪŋ〕*adj.* 失蹤的
be busy + (in) V-ing 忙著～

27.（ **C** ）W：Hi, I'd like to order a large pizza for delivery.

女：你好，我想要訂一個大披薩外送。

M：What would you like on it?

男：妳上面要放什麼料？

W：Cheese and pepperoni.

女：起司和義大利辣味香腸。

Question：What does the woman want?

　　　　女士要什麼？

A. A small pizza with black olives and onion.

　　一個有黑橄欖和洋蔥的小披薩。

B. A medium pizza with ham and pineapple.

　　一個有火腿和鳳梨的中披薩。

C. A large pizza with cheese and pepperoni.

　　一個有起司跟義大利辣味香腸的大披薩。

* **would like to + V.** 想要～
order〔'ɔrdɚ〕*v.* 訂購；點（菜）　　pizza〔'pitsə〕*n.* 披薩
delivery〔dɪ'lɪvərɪ〕*n.* 遞送；外送
cheese〔tʃiz〕*n.* 起司；乳酪
pepperoni〔͵pɛpə'ronɪ〕*n.* 義大利辣味香腸
olive〔'ɑlɪv〕*n.* 橄欖　　onion〔'ʌnjən〕*n.* 洋蔥
medium〔'midɪəm〕*adj.* 中型的
ham〔hæm〕*n.* 火腿　　pineapple〔'paɪn͵æpl̩〕*n.* 鳳梨

28. (**C**) W：Aren't you excited about the game tomorrow?

女：你對明天的比賽不興奮嗎？

M：Not really. I probably won't even get in the game.
The coach says I'm too short.

男：說不上是興奮，我可能甚至都上不了場。教練說我
太矮。

W：You never know. Think positive!

女：很難說。樂觀點！

Question：How does the man feel about tomorrow's game?

男子對於明天的比賽有什麼感覺？

A. Excited. 興奮的。

B. Nervous. 緊張的。

C. Indifferent. <u>漠不關心的。</u>

* excited (ɪk'saɪtɪd) *adj.* 興奮的
 not really 不完全是；說不上
 probably ('prɑbəblɪ) *adv.* 可能；十之八九
 even ('ivən) *adv.* 甚至
 get in 加入；參與   ***You never know.*** 很難說。
 positve ('pɑzətɪv) *adj.* 樂觀的；積極的
 Think positive! 樂觀點！   nervous ('nɝvəs) *adj.* 緊張的
 indifferent (ɪn'dɪfərənt) *adj.* 漠不關心的

29. (**C**) M：How was your weekend?

男：週末如何？

W：It was great! We had a barbeque on Saturday and
went to the park yesterday.

女：非常棒！我們週六烤肉，昨天去公園。

M：Sounds like you made the most of your time.

男：聽起來你們很會善用時間。

Question : When did this conversation take place?

這對話是發生在何時?

A. On Saturday. 週六。

B. On Sunday. 週日。

C. On Monday. 週一。

* weekend (ˈwikˌɛnd) *n.* 週末 　　barbecue (ˈbɑrbɪˌkju) *n.* 烤肉
sound (saʊnd) *v.* 聽起來 　　***sound like*** ~ 聽起來像是~
make the most of 充分利用;善用

30. (**C**) M : Hi, Gloria. You look excited. What happened?

男:嗨,葛洛莉亞,妳看起來很興奮,發生什麼事了?

W : You'll never believe it. I won fifty thousand dollars in the lottery!

女:你肯定不會相信,我樂透中了五萬元!

M : That's incredible! Good for you. I hope you spend the money wisely.

男:真是太不可思議了!真替妳高興,我希望妳會善用那
筆錢。

Question : Why is Gloria so happy?

為什麼葛洛莉亞這麼高興?

A. She won a bet. 她贏得了賭注。

B. She won a contest. 她贏得了比賽。

C. She won the lottery. 她中了樂透。

* lottery (ˈlɑtərɪ) *n.* 樂透;彩券
incredible (ɪnˈkrɛdəbḷ) *adj.* 令人難以置信的
Good for you. 真替你感到高興。
wisely (ˈwaɪzlɪ) *adv.* 聰明地;明智地
win a bet 贏得賭注;賭贏了
contest (ˈkɑntɛst) *n.* 比賽

國中會考英文聽力 ②

一、辨識句意

本部分共 10 題，每題有三個圖片選項，請聽光碟放音機播出的題目，聽後從試題冊上 A、B、C 圖片中，選出一個最適合的回答。每題播出二遍。

例： （聽） John enjoys taking a bath.
　　 （看）

(A) (B) (C)

正確答案為 C，請在答案紙上塗黑作答。

1.　A.　　　　　　B.　　　　　　C.

2.　A.　　　　　　B.　　　　　　C.

3.

4.

5.

6.

7.

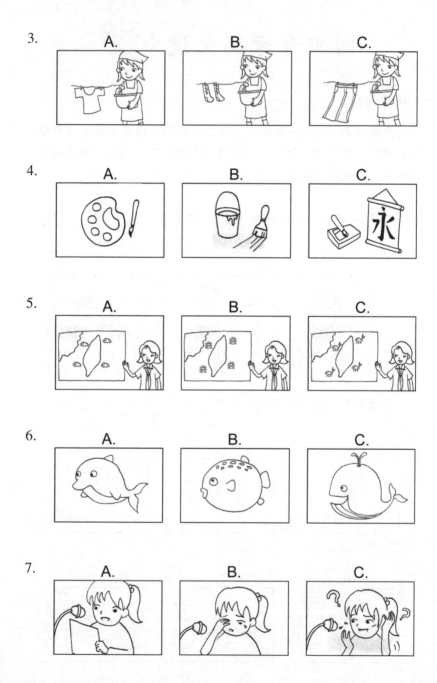

8. A.　　　　B.　　　　C.

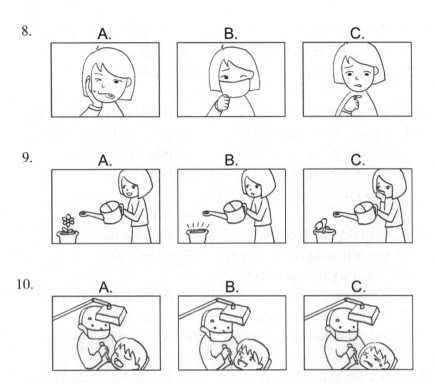

9. A.　　　　B.　　　　C.

10. A.　　　　B.　　　　C.

二、基本問答：選出最適合的回答，完成對話。

本部份共 10 題，每題光碟放音機會播出一個問句或直述句，聽後從試題冊上 A、B、C 三個選項中，選出一個最適合的回答。每題播出二遍。

例： （聽） Hi, Mike. I haven't seen you for a long time. How are you doing?

（看） A. I'm watching TV.
B. I'm OK, thanks.
C. I'm at school.

正確答案為 B，請在答案紙上塗黑作答。

11. A. Seven years old.
    B. I'm doing fine, thanks.
    C. Every morning.

12. A. The baseball stadium.
    B. I heard it's supposed to be sunny.
    C. If not, we can do it tomorrow.

13. A. That depends on how much it weighs.
    B. If you fly on weekdays, it's much cheaper.
    C. All international calls are ten dollars a minute.

14. A. It's Jay Chou, isn't it?
    B. They're very good, aren't they?
    C. He looks good, doesn't he?

15. A. I think they are.
    B. I'm sure they do.
    C. Yes, it is.

16. A. Sooner rather than later.
    B. High and tight.
    C. Medium rare.

17. A. No, I've done it before.
    B. No, I've heard it before.
    C. No, I've been here before.

18. A. Take your time.
    B. Be a sport.
    C. Have a heart.

19. A. At the flower shop on Main Street.
    B. At the library on First Avenue.
    C. At the bakery on Heping East Road.

20. A. No. Sorry, the battery in my phone is dead.
    B. Yes. Leave a message and he'll call you back.
    C. Maybe. It could be out of your reach.

三、言談理解（推論）

　　本部份共 10 題，每題光碟放音機會播出一段對話及一個相關的問題，聽後從試題冊上 A、B、C 三個選項中，選出一個最適合的回答。每題播出二遍。

例： （聽） (Man)　　May I help you?
　　　　　　 (Woman)　Yes, I'd like to look at that red sweater.
　　　　　　　　　　　How much is it?
　　　　　　 (Man)　　It's one thousand dollars.

　　　　　　 Question:　Where are the man and the woman?

（看）　A. In a restaurant.
　　　　B. In the living room.
　　　　C. In a department store.

正確答案為 C，請在答案紙上塗黑作答。

21. A. On a train.
　　B. On a boat.
　　C. In a car.

22. A. It might rain later.
　　B. It is cold outside.
　　C. It is very windy.

23. A. Classmates.
　　B. Co-workers.
　　C. Roommates.

24. A. The man should have better taste.
　　B. The man should have placed his order earlier.
　　C. The man should have to pay extra for delivery.

25. A. Show her proof of identification.
　　B. Pay her taxes.
　　C. Get her driver's license.

26. A. Return the sweater.
　　B. Get the sweater in a larger size.
　　C. Exchange the sweater for a different color.

27. A. He doesn't know how to play chess.
　　B. He can't find anything to wear.
　　C. He's bored.

28. A. Give the man an aspirin.
　　B. Take the man to work.
　　C. Call the doctor.

29. A. A type of vegetable.
　　B. A style of chili.
　　C. A kind of seafood.

30. A. No more than 30 minutes.
　　B. Exactly 30 minutes.
　　C. Almost an hour.

國中會考英文聽力 ② 詳解

一、辨識句意

1. (**A**) Jody is mopping the floor. 茱蒂正在拖地板。

   * mop〔 map〕v. (用拖把) 拖；擦　　floor〔 flor〕n. 地板

2. (**B**) Henry is putting sand into a bucket.
   亨利正在把沙子放進水桶裡。

   * sand〔 sænd〕n. 沙子　　bucket〔'bʌkɪt〕n. 水桶

3. (**B**) Nina has just washed her socks. 妮娜剛洗完襪子。

   * wash〔 wɑʃ〕v. 洗　　socks〔 sɑks〕n. pl. 短襪

4. (**C**) We will study Chinese calligraphy today.
   我們今天要學中文書法。

   * study〔'stʌdɪ〕v. 學習；研讀　　Chinese〔 tʃaɪ'niz〕adj. 中文的
   calligraphy〔 kə'lɪɡrəfɪ〕n. 書法

5. (**C**) The weather in Taiwan is rainy. 台灣的天氣是雨天。

   * weather〔'wɛðɚ〕n. 天氣　　rainy〔'renɪ〕adj. 下雨的

6. (**C**) We visited the aquarium and saw a blue whale.
   我們參觀水族館看到藍鯨。

   * visit〔'vɪzɪt〕v. 參觀
   aquarium〔 ə'kwɛrɪəm〕n. 水族館【複數 aquaria 或 aquariums】
   whale〔 hwel〕n. 鯨魚

7. (**C**) Sally is confused. 莎莉感到困惑。

   * confused〔 kən'fjuzd〕adj. 困惑的

8. (**A**) Margaret has a toothache. 瑪格麗特牙痛。

   * toothache〔'tuθ,ek〕n. 牙痛

9. (**C**) Laura's flower has died. 蘿拉的花枯萎了。

　　* die〔daɪ〕n.（植物、花）枯萎；（人、動物）死亡

10. (**C**) John is afraid of going to the dentist. 約翰害怕看牙醫。

　　* *be afriad of + V-ing* 害怕～　　dentist〔'dɛntɪst〕n. 牙醫
　　 go to the dentist 去牙醫診所

二、基本問答

11. (**B**) Good morning, Harry. How are you? 早安，亨利。你好嗎？

　　A. Seven years old. 七歲大。
　　B. I'm doing fine, thanks. 我很好，謝謝。
　　C. Every morning. 每天早上。

　　* *be doing fine* 過得好

12. (**B**) Today's the big game. I hope it doesn't rain. Do you know
　　the forecast?

　　今天有場盛大的比賽，我希望不會下雨。你有看天氣預報嗎？

　　A. The baseball stadium. 在棒球場。
　　B. I heard it's supposed to be sunny. 我聽說應該是晴天。
　　C. If not, we can do it tomorrow.
　　　　如果不行的話，我們可以明天做。

　　* forecast〔for'kæst〕n. 預測；預報
　　 stadium〔'stedɪəm〕n.（戶外）運動場；體育場
　　 suppose〔sə'poz〕v. 認為　　sunny〔'sʌnɪ〕adj. 晴朗的

13. (**A**) I'd like to send this letter to the U.S. by airmail. How much
　　will it cost? 我想要用航空郵寄把這封信寄到美國，費用是多少？

　　A. That depends on how much it weighs.
　　　　那要看這封信有多重。
　　B. If you fly on weekdays, it's much cheaper.
　　　　如果你搭平日班機，會便宜很多。

C. All international calls are ten dollars a minute.
所有的國際電話都是一分鐘十元。

would like to + V. 想要～　　send〔sɛnd〕v. 寄；送
letter〔ˈlɛtɚ〕n. 信　　airmail〔ˈɛr,mel〕n. 航空郵政
by airmail 以航空郵寄　　cost〔kɔst〕v. (事物) 花費
depend on 取決於　　weigh〔we〕v. 重～
fly〔flaɪ〕v. 搭飛機
much〔mʌtʃ〕adv. (修飾比較級) 大大地；非常
cheap〔tʃip〕adj. 便宜的
international〔,ɪntɚˈnæʃənl〕adj. 國際的
international call 國際電話

14. (**A**) Oh, I love this song! Do you know who sings it?
哦，我愛這首歌！你知道是誰唱的嗎？

A. It's Jay Chou, isn't it? 是周杰倫，不是嗎？
B. They're very good, aren't they? 他們很棒，不是嗎？
C. He looks good, doesn't he? 他看起來很棒，不是嗎？

* look〔lʊk〕v. 看起來

15. (**C**) Look! There's Jimmy. Is that his new girlfriend?
你看！吉米在那裡。那是他的新女朋友嗎？

A. I think they are. 我覺得他們是。
B. I'm sure they do. 我確定他們是。
C. Yes, it is. 是的，沒錯。

* look〔lʊk〕v. 看；瞧【用於引起對方的注意】
girlfriend〔ˈgɝl,frɛnd〕n. 女朋友　　sure〔ʃʊr〕adj. 確定的

16. (**C**) Dad's making steaks on the grill tonight. How would you
like yours done? 爸爸今晚要烤牛排，你要幾分熟？

A. Sooner rather than later. 越早越好。
B. High and tight. 平頭。
C. Medium rare. 三分熟。

* steak〔stek〕*n.* 牛排
How would you like your steak done? 你要幾分熟的牛排？
sooner rather than later 越早越好（= *as soon as possible*）
high and tight （髮型）平頭（= *crew cut*）．
medium rare （牛排）三分熟

17. (**C**) Welcome to Taiwan.　Is this your first visit?
歡迎來到台灣，這是你第一次來嗎？
A. No, I've done it before. 不，我之前做過了。
B. No, I've heard it before. 不，我之前聽過了。
C. No, I've been here before. <u>不，我之前來過了。</u>
* visit〔'vɪzɪt〕*n.* 參觀；探訪　　***have been* (*to*)** ~　曾經去過~

18. (**A**) I need to change my shirt.　Do you mind waiting?
我需要把襯衫換掉，你介意等我嗎？
A. Take your time. <u>慢慢來。</u>
B. Be a sport. 夠朋友點。【詳見背景說明】
C. Have a heart. 發發慈悲。【詳見背景說明】
* shirt〔ʃɝt〕*n.* 襯衫　　mind〔maɪnd〕*v.* 介意
wait〔wet〕*v.* 等待　　***mind* + *V-ing*** 介意…
take* one's *time 從容~；慢慢地~
sport〔sport〕*n.* 樂於助人的人；隨和的人
Be a sport. 夠朋友點；講點義氣。(= *Be a good friend.*
= *Be nice.*)　　heart〔hɑrt〕*n.* 同情心
Have a heart. 發發慈悲；行行好吧。(= *Be nice*)

19. (**C**) The cake was delicious, Jessie.　Where did you get it?
潔西，蛋糕很好吃。妳在哪買的？
A. At the flower shop on Main Street. 在主街上的花店。
B. At the library on First Avenue. 在第一大道的的圖書館。
C. At the bakery on Heping East Road.
<u>在和平東路的麵包店。</u>

* cake〔kek〕*n.* 蛋糕　　delicious〔dɪˈlɪʃəs〕*adj.* 美味的
get〔gɛt〕*v.* 買　　***flower shop*** 花店
main〔men〕*adj.* 主要的
Main Street （小城鎮的）大街；主要街道
library〔ˈlaɪˌbrɛrɪ〕*n.* 圖書館　　avenue〔ˈævəˌnu〕*n.* 大道
bakery〔ˈbekərɪ〕*n.* 麵包店　　east〔ist〕*n.* 東；東方

20. (**A**) I've been trying to reach you all day. Did you get my
message?　我整天試著要聯絡上你，你有收到我的訊息嗎？

　A. No. Sorry, the battery in my phone is dead.

　　　沒有，抱歉，我手機電池沒電了。

　B. Yes. Leave a message and he'll call you back.

　　　有，請留言，他會回你電話。

　C. Maybe. It could be out of your reach.

　　　或許。它可能在你拿不到的地方。

* reach〔ritʃ〕*v.* （用電話）聯絡　*n.* 伸手可及的範圍
message〔ˈmɛsɪdʒ〕*n.* 訊息；留言　　battery〔ˈbætərɪ〕*n.* 電池
dead〔dɛd〕*adj.* （電池）沒電的
leave a message 留言　　***call sb. back*** 回電話給某人
maybe〔ˈmebi〕*adv.* 可能；或許
out of one's reach 在某人拿不到的地方；非某人能力所及

三、言談理解

21. (**C**) M：Did you hear that? It sounded like we hit something.
I hope it wasn't an animal.

　　男：妳有聽到嗎？聽起來好像我們撞到某個東西，我希望不會
　　　　是隻動物。

　　W：No. We have a flat tire.

　　女：不是，是爆胎了。

　　M：Good thing we have a spare.【詳見背景說明】

　　男：幸好我們有備胎。

Question : Where are the speakers?　說話者在哪裡？

A. On a train.　在火車上。　　B. On a boat.　在船上。

C. In a car.　在車子裡。

* sound〔saʊnd〕*v.* 聽起來　　***it sounds like*** 聽起來似乎～

hit〔hɪt〕*v.* 撞到　　animal〔'ænəmḷ〕*n.* 動物

flat〔flæt〕*adj.* 平的；沒氣的　　tire〔taɪr〕*n.* 輪胎

flat tire 爆胎

Good thing (***that***)... 幸好；還好 (= *It's a good thing* (*that*)...)

spare〔spɛr〕*n.* 備用輪胎 (= *spare tire*)　　boat〔bot〕*n.* 船

22. (**A**) W : How cold is it out there?

女：外面有多冷？

M : It's not too bad.　But you might want to bring an
umbrella.

男：不會太冷，但是妳可能要帶把雨傘。

W : Oh, is it supposed to rain later?

女：喔，待會會下雨嗎？

Question : What does the man imply?　男士暗示什麼？

A. It might rain later.　待會可能會下雨。

B. It is cold outside.　外面很冷。

C. It is very windy.　風很大。

* ***out there*** 外面 (= *outside*)

bad〔bæd〕*adj.* (天氣) 惡劣的；壞的

umbrella〔ʌm'brɛlə〕*n.* 雨傘　　suppose〔sə'poz〕*v.* 認為

rain〔ren〕*v.* 下雨　　later〔'letɚ〕*adv.* 後來；之後

imply〔ɪm'plaɪ〕*v.* 暗示　　outside〔'aʊt'saɪd〕*adv.* 在外面

windy〔'wɪndɪ〕*adj.* 多風的；颱風的

23. (**B**) W : Where can we hold our meeting?

女：哪裡可以舉辦會議？

M : How about in the conference room?

男：在會議室如何？

W：That won't work. The sales department is using it all day.

女：那行不通，銷售部門整天都會使用那裡。

Question：What is the most probable relationship between the speakers? 這兩個說話者最可能是什麼關係？

A. Classmates. 同班同學。

B. Co-workers. 同事。

C. Roommates. 室友。

* hold〔hod〕v. 舉行；召開（會議等）
  meeting〔'mitɪŋ〕n. 會議　conference〔'kɑnfərəns〕n. 會議
  conference room 會議室　work〔wɜk〕v. 行得通
  sales〔selz〕adj. 銷售的　department〔dɪ'pɑrtmənt〕n. 部門
  probable〔'prɑbəbḷ〕adj. 可能的
  relationship〔rɪ'leʃən,ʃɪp〕n. 關係
  co-worker〔'ko,wɜkə〕n. 同事

24.（ **B** ）M：Can you have the flowers delivered tomorrow morning?

男：你明天可以把花送到嗎？

W：Well, tomorrow being Mother's Day, sir, I can't guarantee it. We process our orders as they come in. The flowers will get there at some point tomorrow.

女：嗯，先生，明天是母親節，我不能保證可以做到。我們依照接單的順序處理。花會在明天的某個時候送達。

M：How about if I pay extra?

男：那如果我多付點錢呢？

Question：What does the woman imply? 女士暗示什麼？

A. The man should have better taste.
　男士應該有好一點的品味。

B. The man should have placed his order earlier.
　男士應該早一點下訂單。

C. The man should have to pay extra for delivery.
　　男士應該多付點運費。

* deliver〔dɪ'lɪvə〕v. 遞送　　***Mother's Day*** 母親節
　garuantee〔͵gærən'ti〕v. 保證　　process〔'prɑsɛs〕v. 處理
　order〔'ɔrdə〕n. 訂貨；訂單　　***come in*** 到達；被收到
　point〔pɔɪnt〕n. 時候；時刻　　extra〔'ɛkstrə〕*adv.* 額外地
　taste〔test〕n. 品味　　***place*** one's ***order*** 下訂單；訂購
　delivery〔dɪ'lɪvərɪ〕n. 遞送

25. (**C**) W：Yes, I'd like to apply for my driver's license.
　　　女：是的，我想要申請駕照。
　　　M：Take this number, fill out this form, and wait in that line
　　　　　until your number is called.
　　　男：拿這張號碼牌，填這個表格，然後去那裡排隊直到叫到妳的
　　　　　號碼。
　　　W：Will I need to show proof of identification?
　　　女：我需要出示任何身份證明嗎？
　　　Question：What does the woman want to do?
　　　　　　　女士想要做什麼？
　　　A. Show her proof of identification. 出示她的身份證明。
　　　B. Pay her taxes. 繳稅。
　　　C. Get her driver's license. 取得駕照。
　　　* ***would like to*** + V. 想要～　　apply〔ə'plaɪ〕v. 申請 <*for*>
　　　license〔'laɪsn̩s〕n. 執照　　***driver's license*** 駕駛執照
　　　fill out 填寫　　form〔fɔrm〕n. 表格
　　　line〔laɪn〕n. 列；排　　***wait in line*** 排隊
　　　show〔ʃo〕v. 出示　　proof〔pruf〕n. 證明
　　　identification〔aɪ͵dɛntəfə'keʃən〕n. 身份證明
　　　tax〔tæks〕n. 稅

26. (**A**) M：I'd like to return this sweater.
　　　男：我想要退還這件毛衣。

W：What's wrong with it? Too small? Too big? Wrong color?

女：有什麼問題嗎？太小？太大？顏色不對？

M：No, the sweater is fine. I just don't wear sweaters.

男：不，這件毛衣很好，我只是不穿毛衣。

Question：What does the man want to do?

男士想要做什麼？

A. Return the sweater. 退還毛衣。

B. Get the sweater in a larger size. 買尺寸大一點的毛衣。

C. Exchange the sweater for a different color.

換另一個顏色的毛衣。

* return〔rɪ'tɝn〕v. 退還　　sweater〔'swɛtɚ〕n. 毛衣

What's wrong with it? 有什麼問題嗎？

color〔'kʌlɚ〕n. 顏色　　size〔saɪz〕n. 尺寸

exchange〔ɪks'tʃendʒ〕v. 退換

exchange A ***for*** B　用 A 換 B

27. (**C**) M：I'm so bored. There isn't anything to do.

男：我好無聊，沒事可做。

W：Do you want to play a game? How about chess?

女：你要不要玩場遊戲？西洋棋如何？

M：Chess? Ugh. That's even worse than doing nothing at all.

男：西洋棋？啊，那比什麼都不做還糟。

Question：What is the man's problem? 男士有什麼問題？

A. He doesn't know how to play chess.

他不知道怎麼下西洋棋。

B. He can't find anything to wear. 他找不到可穿的衣服。

C. He's bored. 他很無聊。

* bored〔bɔrd〕*adj.* 無聊的　　game〔gem〕*n.* 遊戲；比賽
  How about ~ ? ～如何？　　chess〔tʃɛs〕*n.* 西洋棋
  ugh〔ʌg〕*interj.*（表示厭惡、輕蔑等）啊！；唉呀！
  even〔'ivən〕*adv.*（用於修飾比較級）更　　wear〔wɛr〕*v.* 穿；戴

28. (**C**) W：I'm not going to work today.　I feel terrible.

    女：我今天不去工作了，我覺得很難受。

    M：What's wrong?　Do you have a fever?　Should I call
    the doctor?

    男：怎麼了？發燒了嗎？要我叫醫生嗎？

    W：Maybe.　My throat is sore and my head hurts.

    女：或許，我喉嚨痛，頭也痛。

    Question：What will the man most likely do next?

    　　　　男士接下來最有可能做什麼？

    A.　Give the man an aspirin. 給男士阿斯匹靈。

    B.　Take the man to work. 帶男士去工作。

    C.　Call the doctor. <u>叫醫生。</u>

    * terrible〔'tɛrəbḷ〕*adj.* 難受的
      ***What's wrong** (**with you**)?* 怎麼了？
      fever〔'fivɚ〕*n.* 發燒　　throat〔θrot〕*n.* 喉嚨
      sore〔sor〕*adj.* 痛的；發炎的
      have a sore throat 喉嚨痛　　hurt〔hɝt〕*v.* 疼痛
      aspirin〔'æspərɪn〕*n.* 阿斯匹靈【解熱疼痛藥】
      call the doctor （打電話）叫醫生

29. (**C**) M：Our soup today is clam chowder.

    男：我們今天的湯是蛤蜊巧達濃湯。

    W：I'm allergic to seafood.

    女：我對海鮮過敏。

    M：In that case, why don't you try the Texas-style chili?

    男：那樣的話，妳何不嘗試德州風味紅辣椒？

Question : What is a clam? clam 是什麼？

A. A type of vegetable. 一種蔬菜。

B. A style of chili. 一種辣椒。

C. A kind of seafood. 一種海鮮。

* soup〔sup〕n. 湯　　clam〔klæm〕n. 蛤蜊
  chowder〔'tʃaudə〕n. 羹湯　　***clam chowder*** 蛤蜊巧達濃湯
  allergic〔ə'lɜdʒɪk〕adj. 過敏的
  be allergic to 對⋯過敏　　seafood〔'si,fud〕n. 海鮮
  Texas〔'tɛksəs〕n. 德州【位於美國西南部】
  style〔staɪl〕n. 風格　　***in that case*** 那樣的話
  chili〔'tʃɪlɪ〕n. 紅辣椒　　vegetable〔'vɛdʒtəbl̩〕n. 蔬菜

30. (**A**) M : Did it take you a long time to write your essay?

男：妳花很長的時間寫妳的文章嗎？

W : Not at all. I spent maybe half an hour on it, tops.

女：一點也不，我大概最多只花半個小時。

M : Really? Mine took forever.

男：真的嗎？我花很久才寫完。

Question : How much time did the woman spend writing
　　　　　her essay? 女士花了多少時間寫她的文章？

A. No more than 30 minutes. 最多三十分鐘。

B. Exactly 30 minutes. 剛好三十分鐘。

C. Almost an hour. 幾乎一小時。

* take〔tek〕v. 花費（時間、勞力）
  essay〔'ɛse〕n. 論說文；散文　　***not at all*** 一點也不
  tops〔taps〕adv. 最多（= *at most*）
  forever〔fə'ɛvə〕adv. 永久地　　n. 很長一段時間
  take forever 花很長的時間（= *take a very long time*）
  no more than 僅僅；至多
  exactly〔ɪg'zæktlɪ〕adv. 正好；恰好

國中會考英文聽力 ③

一、辨識句意

　　本部分共 10 題，每題有三個圖片選項，請聽光碟放音機播出的題目，聽後從試題冊上 A、B、C 圖片中，選出一個最適合的回答。每題播出二遍。

例：　（聽）　John enjoys taking a bath.
　　　（看）

　　　(A)　　　　　　　(B)　　　　　　　(C)

正確答案為 C，請在答案紙上塗黑作答。

1.　　A.　　　　　　　B.　　　　　　　C.

2.　　A.　　　　　　　B.　　　　　　　C.

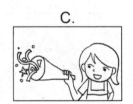

3.

    A.   B.   C.

4.

    A.   B.   C.

5.

    A.   B.   C.

6.

    A.   B.   C.

7.

    A.   B.   C.

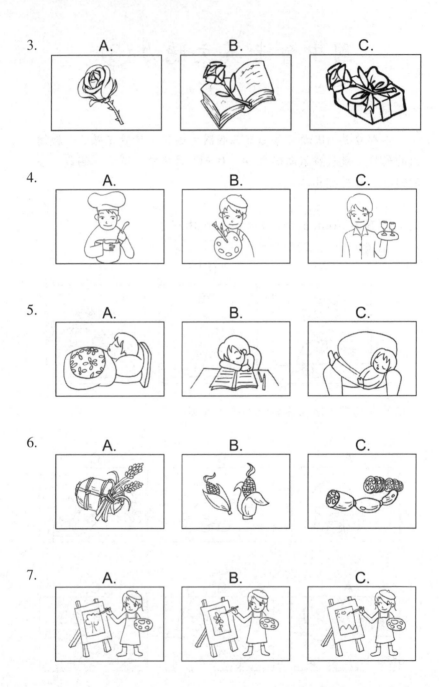

8.

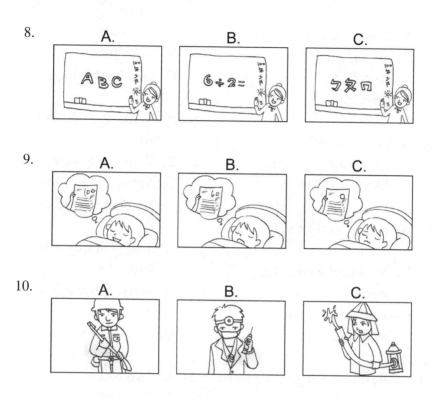

9.

10.

二、基本問答：選出最適合的回答，完成對話。

　　本部份共 10 題，每題光碟放音機會播出一個問句或直述句，聽後從試題冊上 A、B、C 三個選項中，選出一個最適合的回答。每題播出二遍。

例：　（聽）　Hi, Mike. I haven't seen you for a long time.
　　　　　　How are you doing?

　　　（看）　A.　I'm watching TV.
　　　　　　B.　I'm OK, thanks.
　　　　　　C.　I'm at school.

　　正確答案為 B，請在答案紙上塗黑作答。

11. A. School gets out at 3:00.
    B. No, my plans were cancelled.
    C. Have fun!

12. A. Once a month.
    B. It's cheaper at night.
    C. About NT$350.

13. A. Yes, he said he's stuck in traffic.
    B. No, I kept a copy for myself.
    C. Yes, I called him this morning.

14. A. Never. It's right over there.
    B. Sure. What can I do for you?
    C. Likewise, I'm sure.

15. A. Her name is Lulu.
    B. She's a poodle.
    C. Don't mention it.

16. A. No, it won't.
    B. At 9:00.
    C. I don't take drugs.

17. A. None. Paul drank it all.
    B. Yeah. Help yourself.
    C. Always. I'm a big fan of orange juice.

18. A. Sure. I'll ride with you.
    B. Sorry. My car is in the shop.
    C. No. We'll take mine.

19. A. Two feet.
    B. Seven miles.
    C. Twelve pounds.

20. A. It was supposed to start five minutes ago.
    B. My teacher is here.
    C. I'd rather play violin.

三、言談理解（推論）

　　本部份共 10 題，每題光碟放音機會播出一段對話及一個相關的問題，聽後從試冊上 A、B、C 三個選項中，選出一個最適合的回答。每題播出二遍。

例： （聽）(Man)   May I help you?

(Woman)   Yes, I'd like to look at that red sweater.
How much is it?

(Man)   It's one thousand dollars.

Question: Where are the man and the woman?

（看）A. In a restaurant.

B. In the living room.

C. In a department store.

正確答案為 C，請在答案紙上塗黑作答。

21. A. An estimate.
    B. A ride home.
    C. A new motorcycle.

22. A. Have a meeting.
    B. Go to the airport.
    C. Meet his uncle.

23. A. He's quite smart.
    B. He's frequently lazy.
    C. He's very busy.

24. A. In a bank.
    B. In a department store.
    C. In a restaurant.

25. A. Greet her customers.
    B. Move his bicycle.
    C. Block the entrance.

26. A. One of their classmates.
    B. A school policy.
    C. Their plans for lunch.

27. A. Babysit.
    B. Play golf.
    C. Go to a bridal shower.

28. A. They are tolerant.
    B. They are against it.
    C. They are strict.

29. A. Sell something.
    B. Buy something.
    C. Find a job.

30. A. To transfer the call.
    B. To take a message.
    C. To find Rusty.

國中會考英文聽力 ③ 詳解

一、辨識句意

1. (**B**) Glenda is looking through a telescope.
   格蘭達正透過望遠鏡看東西。
   * ***look through*** 透過⋯看　　telescope〔'tɛlə,skop〕*n.* 望遠鏡

2. (**B**) Martin is using a pair of scissors.　馬丁正在使用剪刀。
   * pair〔pɛr〕*n.*（用於成雙成對的東西）一把；一副
   scissors〔'sɪzəz〕*n. pl.* 剪刀

3. (**C**) Happy birthday! I bought you a gift.
   生日快樂！我買了禮物給你。
   * bought〔bɔt〕*v.* 買【三態爲：buy-bought-bought】
   gift〔gɪft〕*n.* 禮物

4. (**B**) Daniel is an artist.　丹尼爾是個藝術家。
   * artist〔'ɑrtɪst〕*n.* 藝術家；畫家

5. (**B**) Irene fell asleep while studying.　艾琳在讀書時睡著了。
   * ***fall asleep*** 睡著　　study〔'stʌdɪ〕*v.* 讀書

6. (**B**) Corn is very delicious.　玉米很好吃。
   * corn〔kɔrn〕*n.* 玉米
   delicious〔dɪ'lɪʃəs〕*adj.* 好吃的；美味的

7. (**B**) Amber is painting a flower.　安柏正在畫一朵花。
   * paint〔pent〕*v.* 畫
   flower〔'flauə〕*n.* 花

8. (**A**) Kevin enjoys studying English.　凱文喜歡研讀英文。

　　enjoy + V-ing 喜愛～　　study〔'stʌdɪ〕*v.* 研讀

9. (**A**) Steve had a dream that he got a perfect score on his exam.
史帝夫夢見他考試考滿分。

　　dream〔drim〕n. 夢　　*have a dream* 作夢；夢見
　　perfect〔'pɝfɪkt〕*adj.* 完美的
　　score〔skɔr〕*n.* 分數；成績　　*perfect score* 滿分
　　exam〔ɪg'zæm〕*n.* 考試 (= *examination*)

10. (**C**) Mr. Rogers is a fireman.　羅傑先生是消防員。

　　fireman〔'faɪrmən〕n. 消防員；救火員

二、基本問答

11. (**B**) It's getting late, Debbie.　Aren't you going out tonight?
夜深了，黛比。妳今晚不要外出嗎？

　　A. School gets out at 3:00.　學校三點放學。【詳見背景說明】
　　B. No, my plans were cancelled.　不，我的計畫取消了。
　　C. Have fun!　玩得開心點！

　　late〔let〕adj. 夜深的　　*school gets out* （學校）放學
　　plan〔plæn〕*n.* 計畫　　cancel〔'kænsl〕*v.* 取消
　　have fun 玩得愉快

12. (**C**) My phone bill is too high.　How much do you pay every
month?　我的電話費太高了，你每個月付多少錢？

　　A. Once a month.　一個月一次。
　　B. It's cheaper at night.　晚上比較便宜。
　　C. About NT$350.　大約台幣三百五十元。

　　phone〔fon〕n. 電話　　bill〔bɪl〕*n.* 帳單
　　pay〔pe〕*v.* 支付　　cheap〔tʃip〕*adj.* 便宜的

13. (**A**) I wonder what's keeping Thomas. Has he called this morning? 我想知道是什麼事情耽誤湯瑪姆士了。他今天早上有打過電話來嗎？

    A. Yes, he said he's stuck in traffic. 【詳見背景説明】
　　　有，他說他遇到塞車。

    B. No, I kept a copy for myself.
　　　沒有，我自己留了一份副本。

    C. Yes, I called him this morning.
　　　有，我今天早上有打給他。

    * wonder〔'wʌndɚ〕*adj.* 想知道　　keep〔kip〕*v.* 耽誤
　　　What's keeping sb.? 某人怎麼耽擱了？(= *Why sb. is late?*)
　　　stuck〔stʌk〕*v.* 使停留；阻塞【三態為：stick-stuck-stuck】
　　　be stuck in 困於；陷入　　traffic〔'træfɪk〕*n.* 交通
　　　copy〔'kɑpɪ〕*n.* 副本

14. (**B**) Excuse me, Ron. Do you have a minute?
　　　很抱歉，榮恩。你有空嗎？

    A. Never. It's right over there. 從來沒有，就在那邊。

    B. Sure. What can I do for you?
　　　當然，我能幫你什麼忙？

    C. Likewise, I'm sure. 一樣，我確定。

    * ***Excuse me.*** 對不起；抱歉【用於引起人家注意】
　　　minute〔'mɪnɪt〕*n.* 分鐘；片刻
　　　have a minute 有空
　　　likewise〔'laɪk,waɪz〕*adv.* 同樣地；(表示同意) 一樣
　　　sure〔ʃur〕*adj.* 確信的；有把握的

15. (**A**) What an adorable dog! What's its name?
　　　好可愛的一隻狗！牠叫什麼名字？

    A. Her name is Lulu. 牠的名字叫露露。

    B. She's a poodle. 牠是隻貴賓狗。

    C. Don't mention it. 不客氣。

* adorable〔ə'dorəbl〕*adj.* 可愛的；迷人的
poodle〔'pudl〕*n.* 貴賓狗　　mention〔'mɛnʃən〕*v.* 提及；提到
Don't mention it. 不客氣。

16. (**B**) I need to go to the drugstore. What time do they open?
我需要去藥房，他們幾點開？

　　A. No, it won't. 不，它不會。　　　　B. At 9:00. 九點。

　　C. I don't take drugs. 我不吸毒。

　　* drugstore〔'drʌg,store〕*n.* 藥房　　drug〔drʌg〕*n.* 藥；毒品
take drugs 吸毒

17. (**A**) I'm so thirsty! How much orange juice is left in the fridge?
我好渴！還有多少柳橙汁在冰箱裡？

　　A. None. Paul drank it all. 一滴不剩，保羅喝光了。

　　B. Yeah. Help yourself. 是的，自行取用。

　　C. Always. I'm a big fan of orange juice.
　　　　總是如此，我超愛柳橙汁。

　　* thirsty〔'θɝstɪ〕*adj.* 口渴的　　***orange juice*** 柳橙汁
left〔lɛft〕*adj.* 剩下的　　fridge〔frɪdʒ〕*n.* 冰箱
help *oneself* 自行取用　　fan〔fæn〕*n.* 迷；愛好者

18. (**B**) I'm late for work. Can you give me a ride?
我上班遲到了，你可以載我一程嗎？

　　A. Sure. I'll ride with you. 當然，我跟你一起搭乘。

　　B. Sorry. My car is in the shop.
　　　　抱歉，我的車子在店裡。

　　C. No. We'll take mine. 不行，我們會拿我的。

　　* ***be late for***~ 遲到　　ride〔raɪd〕*n.* 搭乘
give *sb.* ***a ride*** 開車載某人；載某人一程
shop〔ʃɑp〕*n.* 商店；工作場所

19. (**C**) William, you look fantastic! How much weight have you lost? 威廉，你看起來棒透了！你減了多少體重？

    A. Two feet. 兩英尺。

    B. Seven miles. 七英里。

    C. Twelve pounds. 十二磅。

    * look〔luk〕*v.* 看起來   fantastic〔fæn'tæstɪk〕*adj.* 很棒的

    weight〔wet〕*n.* 體重   ***lose weight*** 減重

    feet〔fit〕*n. pl.* 呎；英尺【長度單位，一英尺 (foot) 為 30.3 公分】

    mile〔maɪl〕*n.* 哩；英里【距離單位，一英里為 1.6093 公里】

    pound〔paʊnd〕*n.* 磅【重量單位，一磅為 0.45 公斤】

20. (**A**) Look at the clock! What time is your piano lesson?
看那時鐘！你鋼琴課是幾點？

    A. It was supposed to start five minutes ago.

        應該五分鐘前就開始了。

    B. My teacher is here. 我的老師在這裡。

    C. I'd rather play violin. 我寧可拉小提琴。

    * clock〔klɑk〕*n.* 時鐘   piano〔pɪ'æno〕*n.* 鋼琴

    lesson〔'lɛsn̩〕*n.* 課程   suppose〔sə'poz〕*v.* 認為

    be supposed to *+ V.* 應該~   ***would rather*** *+ V.* 寧可~

    violin〔͵vɪə'lɪn〕*n.* 小提琴

三、言談理解

21. (**A**) W：My motorcycle won't start. Can you fix it?

    女：我的摩托車發不動，你可以修好它嗎？

    M：I don't know. I have to see what's wrong with it first.

    男：我不知道，我得先看看出了什麼問題。

    W：OK, but don't do anything until you give me an estimate. I can't afford any costly repairs.

    女：好的，但是還沒估價前，先不要做任何事。我無法負擔
昂貴的修理費。

Question : What does the woman want? 女士要什麼？

A. An estimate. 估價。

B. A ride home. 載她回家。

C. A new motorcycle. 新的摩托車。

* motorcycle〔'motɚ͵saɪkl̩〕*n.* 摩托車
　start〔stɑrt〕*v.*（機車、汽車）發動；起動
　fix〔fɪks〕*v.* 修理　　***what's wrong with ~***　~有什麼問題
　estimate〔'ɛstəmɪt〕*n.* 估價
　afford〔ə'fɔrd〕*v.* 買得起；負擔得起
　costly〔'kɔstlɪ〕*adj.* 昂貴的
　repairs〔rɪ'pɛrz〕*n. pl.* 修理作業
　ride〔raɪd〕*n.* 搭乘

22.（ **A** ）M : Would you be able to meet my uncle at the airport on Tuesday?

　　　男：妳週二能夠在機場接我伯父嗎？

　　　W : Sure.　What time does his flight come in?

　　　女：當然可以，他飛機幾點到達？

　　　M : At 3:30.　I would pick him up myself but I have an important meeting all afternoon.

　　　男：三點三十分，我本來要自己去接他，但是我整個下午有個重要的會議。

　　　Question : What will the man do on Tuesday?

　　　　　　　男士週二要做什麼？

A. Have a meeting. 開會。

B. Go to the airport. 去機場。

C. Meet his uncle. 接他的伯父。

* ***be able to + V.*** 能夠~　　airport〔'ɛr͵port〕*n.* 機場
　flight〔flaɪt〕*n.* 班機　　***come in*** 到達
　pick up 接（某人）
　meeting〔'mitɪŋ〕*n.* 會議

23. (**C**) W : How do you spend your free time?

女：你如何度過你的空閒時間？

M : Are you kidding? What is that?

男：妳在開玩笑嗎？什麼叫作空閒時間？

W : I know how you feel.

女：我懂你的感受。

Question : What does the man imply? 男士暗示什麼？

A. He's quite smart. 他很聰明。

B. He's frequently lazy. 他常常很懶惰。

C. He's very busy. 他很忙碌。

* spend〔spεnd〕v. 度過（時間、假期）

free time 空閒時間

kid〔kɪd〕v. 開玩笑　　imply〔ɪm'plaɪ〕v. 暗示

quite〔kwaɪt〕adv. 相當

frequently〔'frikwəntlɪ〕adv. 經常

24. (**C**) M : If you're ready to place your order, I'm ready whenever you are.

男：如果你們已準備好要點菜，我隨時待命。

W : Could you give us just another minute?

女：可以再給我們一點時間嗎？

M : Sure. If you have any questions about the menu, don't hesitate to ask.

男：當然，如果你們對菜單有問題，別猶豫，請發問。

Question : Where is this conversation taking place?

這對話發生在哪裡？

A. In a bank. 在銀行裡。

B. In a department store. 在百貨公司裡。

C. In a restaurant. 在餐廳。

* order〔'ɔrdɚ〕 *n.* 點菜　　***place an order*** 點菜
minute〔'mɪnɪt〕 *n.* 一會兒　　menu〔'mɛnju〕 *n.* 菜單
hesitate〔'hɛzə,tet〕 *v.* 猶豫　　***take place*** 發生
restaurant〔'rɛstərənt〕 *n.* 餐廳

25. (**B**) W : Excuse me, sir. You can't your park your bicycle there.

女：先生，很抱歉。你不可以把單車停在那裡。

M : Why not?

男：為什麼不行？

W : It's blocking the entrance to my shop.

女：它會擋住我的商店的入口。

Question : What does the woman want the man to do?

　　　　女士要男士做什麼？

A. Greet her customers. 跟她的顧客問好。

B. Move his bicycle. <u>移動他的單車。</u>

C. Block the entrance. 擋住入口。

* park〔pɑrk〕 *v.* 停（車）
bicycle〔'baɪ,sɪkl̩〕 *n.* 單車；腳踏車
block〔blɑk〕 *v.* 阻擋；阻塞
entrance〔'ɛntrəns〕 *n.* 入口；大門
shop〔ʃɑp〕 *n.* 商店　　greet〔grit〕 *v.* 向…問候
customer〔'kʌstəmɚ〕 *n.* 顧客　　move〔muv〕 *v.* 移動

26. (**B**) M : Are students allowed to leave campus during lunch?

男：學生可以在午餐時間離開校園嗎？

W : Not anymore. They changed the rule last year.

女：再也不行了，他們去年改變規定了。

M : So I guess your options are either bring your lunch
from home or eat in the cafeteria?

男：所以我想妳的選擇不是自己從家裡帶便當，就是在自助
餐廳用餐？

Question : What are the speakers discussing?
　　　　　說話者在討論什麼？

A. One of their classmates. 其中一位同學。

B. A school policy. 一個學校的政策。

C. Their plans for lunch. 他們的午餐計畫。

* allow〔əˋlaʊ〕*v.* 允許　　campus〔ˋkæmpəs〕*n.* 校園
　rule〔rul〕*n.* 規定　　option〔ˋɑpʃən〕*n.* 選擇
　either A *or* B　不是 A 就是 B
　cafeteria〔͵kæfəˋtɪrɪə〕*n.* 自助餐廳　　discuss〔dɪˋskʌs〕*v.* 討論
　classmate〔ˋklæs͵met〕*n.* 同班同學
　policy〔ˋpɑləsɪ〕*n.* 政策

27. (**C**) M : Well, looks like we need a babysitter for Saturday night.

男：嗯，看來我們週六晚需要一個保姆。

W : Your sister can't do it?

女：你妹妹不行嗎？

M : No. She's got invited to a bridal shower.

男：不行，她受邀去新娘歡送會。

Question : What will the man's sister do on Saturday night?
　　　　　男士的妹妹週六晚上要做什麼？

A. Babysit　當保姆。

B. Play golf. 打高爾夫球。

C. Go to a bridal shower. 去新娘歡送會。

* *look like*~　看似~
　babysitter〔ˋbebɪ͵sɪtɚ〕*n.* (臨時) 保姆
　bridal〔ˋbraɪdl̩〕*adj.* 新娘的　　shower〔ˋʃaʊɚ〕*n.* 送禮會
　bridal shower　待嫁新娘的禮物贈送會【婚禮前，為慶祝新娘的
　　送禮派對】
　babysit〔ˋbebɪ͵sɪt〕*v.* 當 (臨時) 保姆
　golf〔gɑlf〕*n.* 高爾夫球

28. (**A**)　W：Is it OK to smoke here?

　　　　女：可以在這裡抽煙嗎？

　　　　M：It's against the law to smoke anywhere in public,
　　　　　　but as long as you don't smoke indoors, the police
　　　　　　won't give you a hard time.

　　　　男：在公眾場合抽煙是違法的，但是只要妳不在室內抽煙，
　　　　　　警察就不會找妳麻煩。

　　　　W：Good to know.

　　　　女：知道這樣真是太好了。

　　　Question：What is the attitude of the police toward smoking
　　　　　　　　outside?　警方對於在室外抽煙的態度是什麼？

　　　A.　They are tolerant. <u>他們會容忍。</u>
　　　B.　They are against it.　他們反對。
　　　C.　They are strict.　他們很嚴格。

　　* smoke〔smok〕*v.* 抽煙　　　law〔lɔ〕*n.* 法律
　　against the law　違法的
　　public〔'pʌblɪk〕*adj.* 公共的；大眾的
　　in public　公開地　　**as long as**　只要
　　indoors〔'ɪn'dorz〕*adv.* 在屋內；在室內　　**the police**　警方
　　give *sb.* **a hard time**　讓某人不好過；給某人添麻煩
　　attitude〔'ætə,tud〕*n.* 態度
　　tolerant〔'tɑlərənt〕*adj.* 容忍的；寬容的
　　against〔ə'gɛnst〕*prep.* 反對　　strict〔strɪkt〕*adj.* 嚴格的

29. (**C**)　W：Hi, I'm calling about the sales position.　Is it still
　　　　　　open?

　　　　女：嗨，我來電想詢問銷售員的職位，還有缺嗎？

　　　　M：It is.　Do you have any experience with selling things
　　　　　　over the telephone?

　　　　男：有的，妳有任何電話銷售的經驗嗎？

W：Oh, you mean telemarketing? No. And that's not something I would be interested in.

女：喔，你是指電話銷售？不，那也不是我有興趣的。

Question：What does the woman want to do?

女士想做什麼？

A. Sell something. 賣東西。

B. Buy something. 買東西。

C. Find a job. 找工作。

* sales〔selz〕*adj.* 銷售的　　position〔pə'zıʃən〕*n.* 職位
open〔'opən〕*adj.*（職缺）開放的
experience〔ık'spırıəns〕*n.* 經驗
telemarketing〔ˌtɛlə'markıtıŋ〕*n.* 電話銷售
be interested in 對⋯感興趣

30.（**B**）M：Dusty's Cleaning Service. Dusty speaking.

男：灰塵清理服務，我是灰塵。

W：Hi, I'm looking for Rusty.

女：嗨，我要找生銹。

M：Rusty is on vacation. Can I take a message for him?

男：生銹在休假中，我可以替您留話給他嗎？

Question：What does Dusty offer? 灰塵願意做什麼？

A. To transfer the call. 轉接電話。

B. To take a message. 記錄留言。

C. To find Rusty. 找到生銹。

* dusty〔'dʌstı〕*adj.* 滿是灰塵的
look for 尋找　　rusty〔'rʌstı〕*adj.* 生銹的
on vacation 休假中　　message〔'mɛsıdʒ〕*n.* 留言；訊息
take a messgae 記錄留言
offer〔'ɔfə˞〕*v.* 提供；提議；表示願意
transfer〔træns'fɝ〕*v.* 轉接（電話）

國中會考英文聽力 ④

一、辨識句意

　　本部分共 10 題，每題有三個圖片選項，請聽光碟放音機播出的題目，聽後從試題冊上 A、B、C 圖片中，選出一個最適合的回答。每題播出二遍。

例：　（聽）　John enjoys taking a bath.
　　　（看）

正確答案為 C，請在答案紙上塗黑作答。

1.

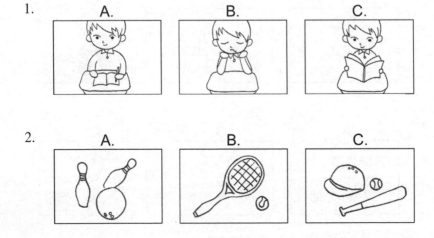

2.

3.

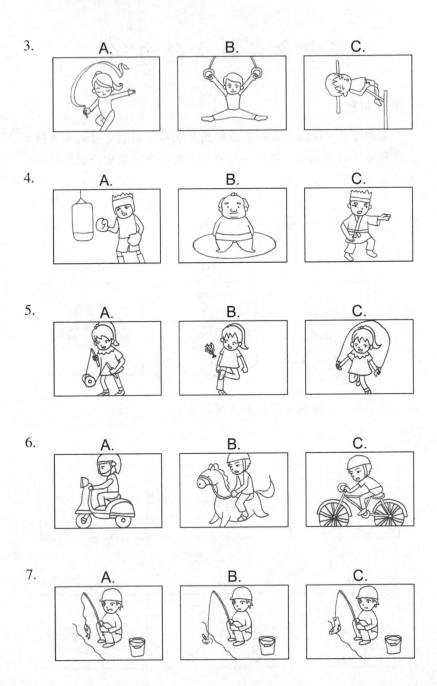

8.

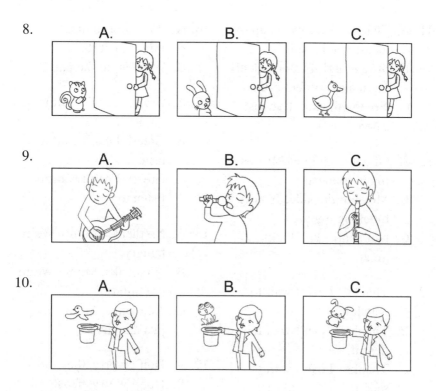

9.

10.

二、基本問答：選出最適合的回答，完成對話。

　　本部份共 10 題，每題光碟放音機會播出一個問句或直述句，
聽後從試題冊上 A、B、C 三個選項中，選出一個最適合的回答。
每題播出二遍。

例：　（聽）　Hi, Mike. I haven't seen you for a long time.
　　　　　　How are you doing?

　　　（看）　A. I'm watching TV.
　　　　　　B. I'm OK, thanks.
　　　　　　C. I'm at school.

　　正確答案為 B，請在答案紙上塗黑作答。

11. A. Thanks. I'd love a cup of tea, if you have it.
　　B. Sure thing! I can drink all night and not feel drunk.
　　C. No, thank you. I've just eaten.

12. A. Of course it does. It's as big as a house.
　　B. Move to the side. You're blocking my view.
　　C. Not at all. You look great.

13. A. Thanks. I can't wait to watch it.
　　B. Thanks. I can't wait to hear it.
　　C. Thanks. I can't wait to read it.

14. A. Yes, I will.
　　B. Yes, I can.
　　C. No, I haven't.

15. A. His name is Rex.
　　B. He's four months old.
　　C. He's a foxhound.

16. A. Way after midnight.
　　B. I didn't get it.
　　C. We went to the park.

17. A. Great! I can't wait to see it.
　　B. Great! I can't wait to taste it.
　　C. Great! I can't wait to listen to it.

18. A. No thanks, Mom. We're hungry.
　　B. No thanks, Mom. We're not thirsty.
　　C. No thanks, Mom. We just ate pizza.

19. A. Don't worry, they did.
　　B. Don't worry, he is.
　　C. Don't worry, I will.

20. A. You're very lucky. He's a generous boyfriend.
　　B. You're much too young. Marriage is for adults.
　　C. You're out of your mind. I can't afford that.

三、言談理解（推論）

　　本部份共 10 題，每題光碟放音機會播出一段對話及一個相關的問題，聽後從試題冊上 A、B、C 三個選項中，選出一個最適合的回答。每題播出二遍。

例： （聽）(Man)　　May I help you?

(Woman)　Yes, I'd like to look at that red sweater. How much is it?

(Man)　　It's one thousand dollars.

Question: Where are the man and the woman?

（看）A. In a restaurant.

B. In the living room.

C. In a department store.

正確答案為 C，請在答案紙上塗黑作答。

21. A. Brother and sister.
    B. Teacher and student.
    C. Husband and wife.

22. A. The neighborhood has remained the same.
    B. The neighborhood has changed.
    C. The neighborhood needs to change.

23. A. Most bank robbers are women.
    B. All men are bank robbers.
    C. It's unusual for a woman to rob a bank.

24. A. Jeffrey didn't clean his room.
    B. Jeffrey didn't do a good job of cleaning his room.
    C. Jeffrey didn't have to clean his room.

25. A. She likes it.
    B. She dislikes it.
    C. She has no opinion.

26. A. He lost weight.
    B. He got a haircut.
    C. He bought new clothes.

27. A. His watch.
    B. His wallet.
    C. His phone.

28. A. In a restaurant.
    B. In a department store.
    C. In a post office.

29. A. Go to the airport.
    B. Go to the bus station.
    C. Go to the train station.

30. A. Go out and party.
    B. Work overtime.
    C. Stay home and read.

國中會考英文聽力 ④ 詳解

一、辨識句意

1. (**C**) Franklin is reading at his desk. 法蘭克林坐在書桌前唸書。
   * read〔rid〕*v.* 閱讀　　desk〔dɛsk〕*n.* 書桌

2. (**C**) My favorite sport is baseball. 我最喜歡的運動是棒球。
   * favorite〔'fevərɪt〕*adj.* 最喜愛的
   sport〔sport〕*n.* 運動　　baseball〔'bes,bɔl〕*n.* 棒球

3. (**B**) Victor enjoys gymnastics. 維多喜歡做體操。
   * enjoy〔ɪn'dʒɔɪ〕*v.* 享受；喜歡
   gymnastics〔dʒɪm'næstɪks〕*n.* 體操

4. (**A**) Quincy enjoys boxing. 昆西喜歡拳擊。
   * boxing〔'bɑksɪŋ〕*n.* 拳擊

5. (**C**) Rachel enjoys jumping rope. 瑞秋喜歡跳繩。
   * *enjoy + V-ing* 喜歡~　　jump〔dʒʌmp〕*v.* 跳
   rope〔rop〕*n.* 繩子　　*jump rope* 跳繩

6. (**B**) Tommy enjoys horseback riding. 湯米喜歡騎馬。
   * horseback〔'hɔrs,bæk〕*n.* 馬背
   horseback riding 騎馬

7. (**A**) Justin caught a fish. 賈斯丁抓到一隻魚。
   * catch〔kætʃ〕*v.* 抓；捕捉【三態爲：catch-caught-caught】
   fish〔fɪʃ〕*n.* 魚

8. (**C**) There's a duck in Olivia's house. 奧莉薇家裡有隻鴨子。
   * duck〔dʌk〕*n.* 鴨子

9. (**B**) Gary is a talented singer. 蓋瑞是個有天分的歌手。

　　* talented〔'tæləntɪd〕*adj.* 有天分的
　　singer〔'sɪŋɚ〕*n.* 歌手

10. (**C**) The magician made a rabbit appear from his hat.
　　魔術師從他的帽子變出一隻兔子。

　　* magician〔mə'dʒɪʃən〕*n.* 魔術師　　rabbit〔'ræbɪt〕*n.* 兔子
　　appear〔ə'pɪr〕*v.* 出現　　hat〔hæt〕*n.* 帽子

二、基本問答

11. (**A**) Welcome to my home. Please come in. Can I get you
　　something to drink?
　　歡迎來到我家，請進。讓我拿點喝的給你好嗎？

　　A. Thanks. I'd love a cup of tea, if you have it.
　　　<u>謝謝，我想要一杯茶，如果你有的話。</u>
　　B. Sure thing! I can drink all night and not feel drunk.
　　　當然！我可以喝整晚都不醉。
　　C. No, thank you. I've just eaten.
　　　不，謝謝你，我剛吃飽。

　　* drink〔drɪŋk〕*v.* 喝；喝酒　　tea〔ti〕*n.* 茶
　　sure thing 的確；當然　　drunk〔drʌŋk〕*adj.* 酒醉的

12. (**C**) Honey, tell me the truth. Does this dress make me look fat?
　　親愛的，跟我說實話，這件洋裝讓我看起來很胖嗎？

　　A. Of course it does. It's as big as a house.
　　　當然，它跟房子一樣大。
　　B. Move to the side. You're blocking my view.
　　　移到旁邊去，你擋到了我的視線。
　　C. Not at all. You look great.
　　　<u>一點也不，妳看起來很棒。</u>

* honey〔ˈhʌnɪ〕*n.* 親愛的　　truth〔truθ〕*n.* 實話
tell the truth 說實話　　dress〔drɛs〕*n.* 洋裝
fat〔fæt〕*adj.* 肥胖的　　***of course*** 當然
move〔muv〕*v.* 移動　　side〔saɪd〕*n.* 旁邊
block〔blɑk〕*v.* 阻礙；阻擋　　view〔vju〕*n.* 視線
not at all 一點也不　　look〔lʊk〕*v.* 看起來
great〔gret〕*adj.* 很棒的

13. (**C**) Here's that book you asked for. I hope you like it.
這是你要的書。希望你喜歡。

　　A. Thanks. I can't wait to watch it.
　　　謝謝，我等不及要觀賞了。

　　B. Thanks. I can't wait to hear it 謝謝，我等不及要聽了。

　　C. Thanks. I can't wait to read it. <u>謝謝，我等不及要讀了。</u>

　　* ***ask for*** 要求　　***can't wait to + V.*** 等不及～

14. (**C**) This is delicious. Have you ever tried caviar?
這很好吃，你試過魚子醬嗎？

　　A. Yes, I will. 是，我會。

　　B. Yes, I can. 是，我可以。

　　C. No, I haven't. <u>不，我沒試過。</u>

　　* delicious〔dɪˈlɪʃəs〕*adj.* 美味的；好吃的
　　caviar〔ˌkævɪˈɑr〕*n.* 魚子醬

15. (**A**) That's a cute puppy. What's his name?
那隻小狗真可愛，牠叫什麼名字？

　　A. His name is Rex. <u>牠叫雷克斯。</u>

　　B. He's four months old. 牠四個月大了。

　　C. He's a foxhound. 牠是隻獵狐犬。

　　* puppy〔ˈpʌpɪ〕*n.*（未滿一歲的）小狗
　　foxhound〔ˈfɑksˌhaʊnd〕*n.* 獵狐犬

16. (**A**) You're up, finally. What time did you get in last night?

　　你終於起床了。你昨晚幾點回到家?

　　A. Way after midnight. 午夜之後。【詳見背景説明】

　　B. I didn't get it. 我不了解。

　　C. We went to the park. 我們去公園。

　　* ***be up*** 起床　　finally (ˈfaɪnl̩ɪ) *adv.* 最後;終於

　　get in 回家　　way (we) *adv.* (強調) 非常

　　midnight (ˈmɪdˌnaɪt) *n.* 午夜　　***get it*** 了解

17. (**C**) Here's that Lady Gaga CD you wanted to borrow. Just
return it when you're finished with it.

　　這是你要借的女神卡卡的 CD,聽完之後歸還就可以了。

　　A. Great! I can't wait to see it. 太棒了!我等不及要看了。

　　B. Great! I can't wait to taste it.

　　　太棒了,我等不及要品嚐了。

　　C. Great! I can't wait to listen to it.

　　　太棒了!我等不及要聽了。

　　* ***Lady Gaga*** 女神卡卡【美國流行女歌手】

　　CD (音樂) 光碟 (= *compact disc*)

　　borrow (ˈbaro) *v.* 借 (入)　　return (rɪˈtɝn) *v.* 歸還

　　finished (ˈfɪnɪʃt) *adj.* 完成的　　***be finished with*** 用完

　　taste (test) *v.* 品嚐　　***listen to*** 聽

18. (**C**) Are you boys hungry? I can make you some sandwiches if
you like.

　　孩子們你們餓了嗎?如果你們要的話,我可以做一些三明治。

　　A. No thanks, Mom. We're hungry.

　　　不,謝謝媽。我們餓了。

　　B. No thanks, Mom. We're not thirsty.

　　　不,謝謝媽。我們不渴。

　　C. No thanks, Mom. We just ate pizza.

　　　不,謝謝媽。我們剛吃了披薩。

* hungry〔ˈhʌŋgrɪ〕*adj.* 飢餓的
sandwich〔ˈsændwɪtʃ〕*n.* 三明治
thirsty〔ˈθɝstɪ〕*adj.* 口渴的　　pizza〔ˈpitsə〕*n.* 披薩

19.(**C**) Be careful and make sure to call when you get there.
要小心，當你到那裡，一定要打電話。

A. Don't worry, they did. 別擔心，他們打了。

B. Don't worry, he is. 別擔心，他是的。

C. Don't worry, I will. 別擔心，我會。

* care〔ˈkɛrfəl〕*adj.* 小心的
make sure to + V. 確定~　　worry〔ˈwɝɪ〕*v.* 擔心

20.(**A**) Look what Terry gave me! A diamond necklace.
看看泰瑞給了我什麼！一條鑽石項鍊。

A. You're very lucky. He's a generous boyfriend.
妳真幸運。他是一個慷慨的男朋友。

B. You're much too young. Marriage is for adults.
妳太年輕了，結婚是大人的事。

C. You're out of your mind. I can't afford that.
妳瘋了，那我負擔不起。

* diamond〔ˈdaɪmənd〕*n.* 鑽石　　necklace〔ˈnɛklɪs〕*n.* 項鍊
lucky〔ˈlʌkɪ〕*adj.* 幸運的　　generous〔ˈdʒɛnərəs〕*adj.* 慷慨的
marriage〔ˈmærɪdʒ〕*n.* 婚姻　　adult〔əˈdʌlt〕*n.* 成人
mind〔maɪnd〕*n.* 心智　　***out of one's mind*** 發瘋
afford〔əˈfɔrd〕*v.* 負擔得起

三、言談理解

21.(**C**) M: Have the kids eaten supper yet?
男：孩子們吃過晚餐了嗎？

W: Yes, they ate when they got home from school.
女：有，他們從學校回到家就吃了。

M：So what are we going to have?

男：那我們要吃什麼。

Question：Who are the speakers? 說話者是什麼身份？

A. Brother and sister. 兄妹。
B. Teacher and student. 師生。
C. Husband and wife. 夫妻。

* kid〔kɪd〕*n.* 小孩　　supper〔'sʌpɚ〕*n.* 晚餐
  husband〔'hʌzbənd〕*n.* 丈夫　　wife〔waɪf〕*n.* 妻子

22.(**B**) M：I don't even recognize the old neighborhood anymore.

男：我連舊時鄰近的一帶都認不出來了。

W：I know. So much has changed. Isn't that bank where the church used to be?

女：我知道，改變了很多。銀行那地方之前不是教堂嗎？

M：No, that was the old fire station. It looks like they kept some of the original building.

男：不，那個是舊的消防站。他們似乎保留了一些原本的建築。

Question：What does the woman think? 女士的想法是什麼？

A. The neighborhood has remained the same.
   鄰近地區還是保持原狀。
B. The neighborhood has changed. 鄰近地區已經變了。
C. The neighborhood needs to change. 鄰近地區需要改變。

* even〔'ivən〕*adv.* 甚至；連　　recognize〔'rɛkəg,naɪz〕*v.* 認出
  neighborhood〔'nebɚ,hʊd〕*n.* 附近地區
  not…anymore 不再…　　change〔tʃendʒ〕*v.* 改變
  bank〔bæŋk〕*n.* 銀行　　church〔tʃɝtʃ〕*n.* 教堂
  fire station 消防站
  original〔ə'rɪdʒən!〕*adj.* 原本的；原初的
  building〔'bɪldɪŋ〕*n.* 建築物
  remain〔rɪ'men〕*v.* 保持　　***the same*** 相同的

23. (**C**) W：Did they ever catch the guy who robbed the bank?

女：他們有抓到搶銀行的人嗎？

M：Actually, it was a woman. The security cameras caught a picture of her face.

男：事實上，是個女的。安全攝影機有拍到她的臉。

W：Wow, a woman bank robber. You don't hear about those every day, do you?【詳見背景說明】

女：哇，是個女銀行搶匪，你不會天天聽到這樣的事吧，不是嗎？

Question：What does the woman imply? 女士暗示什麼？

A. Most bank robbers are women.

大部份的銀行搶匪都是女人。

B. All men are bank robbers.

所有的男人都是銀行搶匪。

C. It's unusual for a woman to rob a bank.

女人搶銀行是不尋常的。

* catch〔kætʃ〕v. 捕捉【三態為：catch-caught-caught】
rob〔rɑb〕v. 搶劫　　bank〔bæŋk〕n. 銀行
actually〔ˋæktʃʊəlɪ〕adv. 實際上；事實上
security〔sɪˋkjʊrətɪ〕n. 安全　　camera〔ˋkæmərə〕n. 攝影機
robber〔ˋrɑbɚ〕n. 強盜　　*hear about* 聽到關於
imply〔ɪmˋplaɪ〕v. 暗示　　unusual〔ʌnˋjuʒʊəl〕adj. 不尋常的

24. (**B**) W：Jeffrey, I thought I told you to clean your room!

女：傑佛瑞，我想我告訴過你要打掃房間！

M：I did clean it, Mom!

男：我真的打掃過了，媽！

W：You call this clean?

女：你這樣叫作有打掃？

Question：What does the woman imply? 女士暗示什麼？

A. Jeffrey didn't clean his room.

傑佛瑞沒有打掃他的房間。

B. Jeffrey didn't do a good job of cleaning his room.

傑佛瑞房間打掃得不好。

C. Jeffrey didn't have to clean his room.

傑佛瑞不需要打掃房間。

* clean〔klin〕*v.* 打掃；清理　　***do + V.*** 真的～；的確～
do a good job 做得好；幹得好　　***have to + V.*** 必須～

25. (**B**) M：How about renting a movie tonight?

男：今晚租個電影來看如何？

W：You want to stay home again? It's Friday night. Let's do something for a change. I'm sick of staying home every weekend.

女：你又想要待在家？今天是週五晚上。我們來做點不一樣的事情，我已經受夠了每個週末都在家。

M：But doing stuff costs money.

男：但是活動需要花錢。

Question：How does the woman feel about the man's suggestion? 女士對於男士的建議覺得如何？

A. She likes it. 她喜歡。

B. She dislikes it. 她不喜歡。

C. She has no opinion. 她沒意見。

* ***How about~?*** ～如何？　　rent〔rɛnt〕*v.* 租
for a change 改變一下；換個口味
be sick of 厭倦　　stuff〔stʌf〕*n.* 東西；事物
cost〔kɔst〕*v.* (事物) 花費
suggestion〔səg'dʒɛstʃən〕*n.* 建議
dislike〔dɪs'laɪk〕*v.* 不喜歡
opinion〔ə'pɪnjən〕*n.* 意見

26. (**B**) W：You look great, Tim. I love the new hairstyle.

女：提姆，你看起來很棒，我喜歡你的新髮型。

M：Thanks, Lisa. It was time for a change.

男：謝謝妳，麗莎。該是改變的時候了。

W：I think you look much more handsome and mature with short hair.

女：我覺得你短髮看起來更英俊而且成熟。

Question：What did the man do? 男士做了什麼？

A. He lost weight. 他減重了。

B. He got a haircut. 他剪頭髮了。

C. He bought new clothes. 他買新衣服了。

* look〔luk〕*v.* 看起來　　hairstyle〔'hɛr,staɪl〕*n.* 髮型
  It is time for ~ 該是~的時候了
  handsome〔'hænsəm〕*adj.* 英俊的
  mature〔mə'tʊr〕*adj.* 成熟的　　weight〔wet〕*n.* 體重
  lose weight 減重　　haircut〔'hɛr,kʌt〕*n.* 理髮
  clothes〔kloz〕*n. pl.* 衣服

27. (**C**) M：Have you seen my cell phone anywhere? I thought I left it on the desk.

男：妳有看到我的手機嗎？我想我遺留在書桌上。

W：I haven't seen it. Why don't you call it?

女：我沒看到，你何不打電話看看？

M：That won't help. It's on silent.

男：那沒有用，手機是靜音模式。

Question：What is the man looking for? 男士在找什麼？

A. His watch. 他的手錶。

B. His wallet. 他的皮夾。

C. His phone. 他的電話。

> *cell phone* 手機　　leave〔liv〕*v.* 遺留
> desk〔dɛsk〕*n.* 書桌　　*Why don't you + V.?* 你何不～？
> help〔hɛlp〕*v.* 有用；有幫助
> silent〔'saɪlənt〕*adj.* 無聲的　　*be on silent* （手機）靜音
> *look for* 尋找　　wallet〔'wɔlɪt〕*n.* 皮夾

28. (**B**) W：What do you think?

　　　　女：你覺得如何？

　　　　M：I like the fit, but yellow really isn't my color.

　　　　男：我喜歡合身，但黃色真的不適合我。

　　　　W：Hmm, let me see. I think we have this shirt in blue.
　　　　　　How about that?

　　　　女：嗯，我看看。我覺得我們買這件襯衫的藍色款如何？

　　　　Question：Where is this conversation taking place?

　　　　　　　　　這對話出現在哪裡？

　　　　A. In a restaurant. 在餐廳裡。

　　　　B. In a department store. <u>在百貨公司裡。</u>

　　　　C. In a post office. 在郵局裡。

　　　　* fit〔fɪt〕*n.* 合身；合身的衣服　　yellow〔'jɛlo〕*n.* 黃色
　　　　Let me see. 讓我想想；讓我看看。
　　　　shirt〔ʃɜt〕*n.* 襯衫　　*How about~?* ～如何？
　　　　restaurant〔'rɛstərənt〕*n.* 餐廳
　　　　department store 百貨公司　　*post office* 郵局

29. (**C**) M：Do you know how much a taxi to the train station
　　　　　　　would cost?

　　　　男：妳知道坐計程車到火車站要多少錢嗎？

　　　　W：Somewhere around NT$100.

　　　　女：大概台幣一百元左右。

　　　　M：That's reasonable. Is it easy to catch one in this area?

　　　　男：那很合理，在這裡要攔到計程車容易嗎？

Question : What does the man want to do?　男士想做什麼？

A.　Go to the airport.　去機場。

B.　Go to the bus station.　去公車站。

C.　Go to the train station.　去火車站。

* taxi〔'tæksɪ〕 *n.* 計程車　　***train station***　火車站
　somwhere〔'sʌm,hwɛr〕 *adv.* 大約；大概
　reasonable〔'riznəbl〕 *adj.* 合理的
　area〔'ɛrɪə〕 *n.* 地方；區域　　airport〔'ɛr,port〕 *n.* 機場
　bus station　公車站

30.（ **C** ）W : What are your plans for the weekend?

　　　　女：你週末有什麼計畫？

　　　　M : I'm going to take it easy.　Maybe catch up on a few
　　　　　　books I've been meaning to read.

　　　　男：我打算輕鬆度過。或許會趕快讀一些我一直想看的書。

　　　　W : That sounds relaxing.　Enjoy!

　　　　女：那聽起來真輕鬆愉快。好好享受吧！

　　　　Question : What does the man want to do this weekend?

　　　　　　　　男士週末打算做什麼？

　　　　A.　Go out and party.　出門去狂歡。

　　　　B.　Work overtime.　加班。

　　　　C.　Stay home and read.　待在家讀書。

　　　　* plan〔plæn〕 *n.* 計畫　　***take it easy***　放輕鬆
　　　　catch up on　趕上（尚未做的事）
　　　　mean〔min〕 *v.* 意圖；打算　　sound〔saʊnd〕 *v.* 聽起來
　　　　relaxing〔rɪ'læksɪŋ〕 *adj.* 輕鬆愉快的
　　　　enjoy〔ɪn'dʒɔɪ〕 *v.* 享受
　　　　party〔'partɪ〕 *v.* 盡情享樂；狂歡（= *have a good time*）
　　　　overtime〔'ovɚ,taɪm〕 *adv.* 超出時間地
　　　　work overtime　加班

國中會考英文聽力 ⑤

一、辨識句意

本部分共 10 題，每題有三個圖片選項，請聽光碟放音機播出的題目，聽後從試題冊上 A、B、C 圖片中，選出一個最適合的回答。每題播出二遍。

例： （聽） John enjoys taking a bath.
　　（看）

(A) (B) (C)

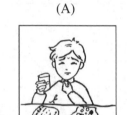  

正確答案為 C，請在答案紙上塗黑作答。

1. A. B. C.

 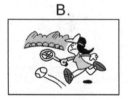 

2. A. B. C.

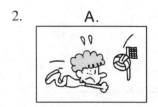  

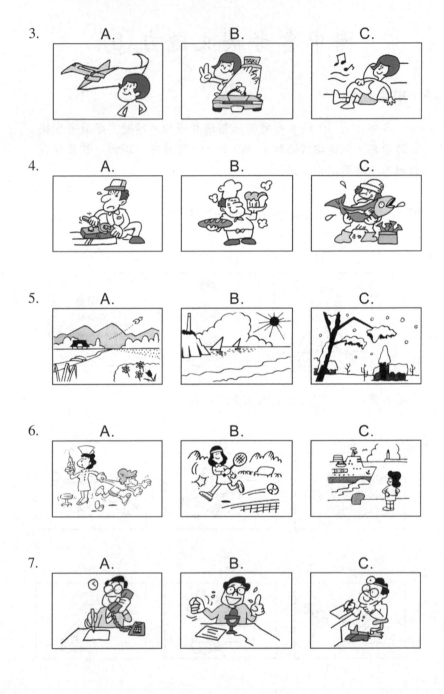

8. A.   B.   C.

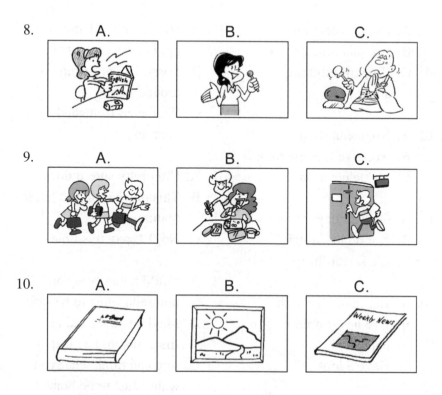

9. A.   B.   C.

10. A.   B.   C.

二、**基本問答**：選出最適合的回答，完成對話。

　　本部份共 10 題，每題光碟放音機會播出一個問句或直述句，聽後從試題冊上 A、B、C 三個選項中，選出一個最適合的回答。每題播出二遍。

例：（聽）Hi, Mike. I haven't seen you for a long time. How are you doing?

（看）　A. I'm watching TV.
　　　　B. I'm OK, thanks.
　　　　C. I'm at school.

正確答案為 B，請在答案紙上塗黑作答。

11. A. I'm on vacation.
　　B. I'm planning on it.
　　C. I'm still thinking about it.

12. A. No, clean it up.
　　B. No, give it some room.
　　C. No, leave it on.

13. A. On Tuesday.
　　B. Not on my watch.
　　C. It's seven-thirty.

14. A. Her name is Sarah.
　　B. I've never used it before.
　　C. Have a look.

15. A. No, thanks. I'm good.
　　B. Who? Beats me.
　　C. Do it. Do it now.

16. A. At the shopping mall.
　　B. About $300.
　　C. That's nice of you.

17. A. His gambling habit is getting out of control.
　　B. Sorry, I'm not from around here.
　　C. We haven't finished counting it yet.

18. A. I'm pretty sure it does.
　　B. This one has all the latest features.
　　C. No, I'll pay this time.

19. A. You'd better bring an umbrella. Just to be safe.
　　B. Maybe you should ask first. Just to be clear.
　　C. You can think what you want. Just to be honest.

20. A. Shh, you'll spoil the surprise.
　　B. I think I left my wallet here last night.
　　C. Put it down before someone gets hurt.

三、言談理解（推論）

　　本部份共 10 題，每題光碟放音機會播出一段對話及一個相關的問題，聽後從試題冊上 A、B、C 三個選項中，選出一個最適合的回答。每題播出二遍。

例： （聽） (Man)　　May I help you?
　　　　　 (Woman)　Yes, I'd like to look at that red sweater.
　　　　　　　　　　How much is it?
　　　　　 (Man)　　It's one thousand dollars.

　　　　　 Question: Where are the man and the woman?

（看） A. In a restaurant.
　　　 B. In the living room.
　　　 C. In a department store.

正確答案爲 C，請在答案紙上塗黑作答。

21. A. On a bus.
　　 B. In a boat.
　　 C. In a car.

22. A. Very well.
　　 B. So-so.
　　 C. Not very well.

23. A. In a butcher shop.
　　 B. In a bakery.
　　 C. In a jewelry store.

24. A. She's not very fond
　　　 of bowling.
　　 B. She's going straight
　　　 home after work.
　　 C. She's working on
　　　 something urgent.

25. A. Her phone was dead.
　　 B. They got lost in
　　　 Evansville.
　　 C. It is impossible to say.

26. A. He changes his mind
　　　 frequently.
　　 B. He can be difficult to work
　　　 with.
　　 C. He talks a lot but does little.

27. A. He didn't have enough
　　　 money.
　　 B. He wasn't in the mood to
　　　 go.
　　 C. He doesn't like Lenny.

28. A. Change his clothes.
　　 B. Make a phone call.
　　 C. Dig a hole.

29. A. Go out for dinner.
　　 B. See a movie.
　　 C. Take a vacation.

30. A. She is a teacher.
　　 B. She is a baseball coach.
　　 C. She is a doctor.

國中會考英文聽力 ⑤ 詳解

一、辨識句意

1. (**C**) Rebecca is at the airport. 瑞貝卡在機場。

    * airport〔'ɛr͵port〕 *n.* 機場

2. (**B**) The boy enjoys watching soccer on TV.
    男孩喜歡看電視足球賽。

    * ***enjoy + V-ing*** 喜歡~　　soccer〔'sɑkɚ〕 *n.* 足球

3. (**B**) Muhammed is a taxi driver. 穆罕默德是個計程車司機。

    * taxi〔'tæksɪ〕 *n.* 計程車　　driver〔'draɪvɚ〕 *n.* 司機；駕駛人

4. (**C**) Mr. Gacy caught a giant fish. 蓋西先生抓到一隻大魚。

    * catch〔kætʃ〕 *v.* 抓；捕捉【三態為：catch-caught-caught】
    giant〔'dʒaɪənt〕 *adj.* 巨大的

5. (**C**) It snows every winter in Canada. 加拿大每個冬天都下雪。

    * snow〔sno〕 *v.* 下雪
    Canada〔'kænədə〕 *n.* 加拿大【位於北美洲北部】

6. (**C**) Janet is waiting for her ship to come in.
    珍妮特在等她的船進港。

    * ***wait for*** 等待　　***come in*** （船）入港；進港

7. (**B**) Leon is a famous radio disc jockey.
    里昂是個有名的電台 DJ。

    * famous〔'feməs〕 *adj.* 有名的　　radio〔'redɪ͵o〕 *n.* 電台
    disc〔dɪsk〕 *n.* 唱片；唱盤（ = *disk*）
    jockey〔'dʒɑkɪ〕 *n.* 操作機器的人
    disc jockey （電台）唱片音樂節目主持人（ = *DJ*）

8. (**B**) Ms. Swift is an excellent public speaker.

　　史威夫小姐是個優秀的公衆演講者。

　　* exellent〔ˈɛksḷənt〕adj. 優秀的
　　public〔ˈpʌblɪk〕adj. 公共的；公衆的
　　speaker〔ˈspikɚ〕n. 演講者

9. (**A**) Polly thinks David is cute.

　　波麗覺得大衛很可愛。

　　* cute〔kjut〕adj. 可愛的

10. (**A**) Please bring that book to me.　請把那本書拿給我。

　　* bring〔brɪŋ〕v. 帶來（給人）

二、基本問答

11. (**C**) Do you have any plans for your summer vacation?

　　你暑假有什麼計畫嗎？

　　A. I'm on vacation.　我在度假。
　　B. I'm planning on it.　我正在擬定它的計畫。
　　C. I'm still thinking about it.　<u>我還在考慮。</u>

　　* vacation〔vəˈkeʃən〕n. 假期
　　　summer vacation 暑假　　***on vacation*** 度假中
　　　plan on 擬定…的計畫　　***think about*** 考慮

12. (**C**) I didn't realize you were studying.　Should I shut off the
　　TV?　我不知道你在唸書，我該關掉電視嗎？

　　A. No, clean it up.　不，把它打掃乾淨。
　　B. No, give it some room.　不，別靠那麼近。【詳見背景說明】
　　C. No, leave it on.　<u>不，讓它開著。</u>

　　* realize〔ˈrɪəˌlaɪz〕v. 知道；了解　　***shut off*** 關掉（電源等）
　　　clean up 清理乾淨　　room〔rum〕n. 空間
　　　leave〔liv〕v. 使保持在（某種狀態）　　on〔ɑn〕adv. 開著

13. (**C**) My watch has stopped. Could you tell me the time?
　　　我的錶停了，可以告訴我現在幾點嗎？

　　　A. On Tuesday. 在星期二。
　　　B. Not on my watch. 在我值班的時候不可以。
　　　C. It's seven-thirty. 七點三十分。

　　　* *the time* 時間；…點…分　　　*on watch* 值班 (= *on duty*)

14. (**A**) That girl looks familiar, doesn't she?
　　　那女孩看起來很面熟，不是嗎？

　　　A. Her name is Sarah. 她的名字叫莎拉。
　　　B. I've never used it before. 我以前從沒用過。
　　　C. Have a look. 看一下。

　　　* familiar〔fəˋmɪljɚ〕*adj.* 熟悉的；面熟的
　　　　have a look 看一看；瞧一瞧

15. (**A**) I'm going to the market. Can I get you anything while I'm
　　　out? 我要去市場，我出去時需要幫你買點什麼嗎？

　　　A. No, thanks. I'm good. 不，謝謝，我很飽。
　　　B. Who? Beats me. 誰？考倒我了。
　　　C. Do it. Do it now. 做，現在就做。

　　　* market〔ˋmɑrkɪt〕*n.* 市場　　　beat〔bit〕*v.* 打敗；難倒
　　　　I'm good. 我很飽。(= *I'm full.*)
　　　　Beats me. 難倒我了；我不知道

16. (**B**) Cool shoes! Do you mind if I ask how much you paid for
　　　them? 好酷的鞋子！介意我問你花了多少錢買的嗎？

　　　A. At the shopping mall. 在購物中心。
　　　B. About $300. 大約三百元。
　　　C. That's nice of you. 你人真好。

　　　* mind〔maɪnd〕*v.* 介意　　　*pay for* 支付
　　　　mall〔mɔl〕*n.* 購物中心　　　*shopping mall* 購物中心

17. (**A**) Eddie looks upset. He must have lost all his money at the casino again. 艾迪看來很沮喪，他一定又在賭場輸光了錢。

    A. His gambling habit is getting out of control.
       <u>他的賭性漸漸失控了。</u>

    B. Sorry, I'm not from around here. 【詳見背景說明】
       很抱歉，我不住這附近。

    C. We haven't finished counting it yet. 我們還沒算完。

    * upset〔ʌpˋsɛt〕*adj.* 不高興的；沮喪的
      must have + p.p. 當時一定～　　　lose〔luz〕*v.* 輸掉
      casino〔kəˋsino〕*n.* 賭場　　　gamble〔ˋgæmbḷ〕*v.* 賭博
      habit〔ˋhæbɪt〕*n.* 習慣　　　***out of control*** 失去控制
      finish + V-ing 結束～　　　count〔kaʊnt〕*v.* 計算

18. (**A**) Does that café have Internet access? I need to check my email. 那間咖啡店有網路嗎？我需要看我的電子郵件。

    A. I'm pretty sure it does. <u>我很確定它有。</u>
    B. This one has all the latest features. 這間有最新的功能。
    C. No, I'll pay this time. 不，這次我付錢。

    * café〔kəˋfe〕*n.* 咖啡店　　　Internet〔ˋɪntəˏnɛt〕*n.* 網際網路
      access〔ˋæksɛs〕*n.* 取得；路徑　　　pretty〔ˋprɪtɪ〕*adv.* 非常
      latest〔ˋletɪst〕*adj.* 最新的　　　feature〔ˋfitʃə〕*n.* 特色；功能
      pay〔pe〕*v.* 支付　　　time〔taɪm〕*n.* 次；回

19. (**A**) Do you think it might rain this afternoon?
    你覺得下午會下雨嗎？

    A. You'd better bring an umbrella. Just to be safe.
       <u>你最好帶支雨傘，為了安全起見。</u>

    B. Maybe you should ask first. Just to be clear.
       或許你應該先問，為了要弄清楚。

    C. You can think what you want. Just to be honest.
       你可以想想你要什麼，誠實就好。

    * safe〔sef〕*adj.* 安全的　　　honest〔ˋɑnɪst〕*adj.* 誠實的

20. (**B**) Hi, Alex. I'm surprised to see you. What brings you here so early in the morning?

嗨，愛力克斯，看到你我很驚訝。為了什麼事早上這麼早來？

A. Shh, you'll spoil the surprise.

噓，你會搞砸了這驚喜。

B. I think I left my wallet here last night.

<u>我覺得我昨晚把皮夾遺留在這裡了。</u>

C. Put it down before someone gets hurt. 【詳見背景說明】

在還沒有人受傷前收手吧。

* surprised〔sə'praɪzd〕*adj.* 驚訝的

　bring〔brɪŋ〕*v.*（事物）引（某人）到某處

　spoil〔spɔɪl〕*v.* 破壞　　wallet〔'wɑlɪt〕*n.* 皮夾

　put down 停止；放下　　***get hurt*** 受傷

三、言談理解

21. (**C**) M：The map says we should get off at the next exit.

男：地圖指出我們應該在下個出口出去。

W：Are you sure? The last sign said "Seattle, 3 miles."

女：你確定嗎？最後一個路標寫著「西雅圖，三英里」。

M：This is a shortcut that will save us a bit of time.

男：這是捷徑，可以幫我們省下一些時間。

Question：Where are the speakers? 說話者在哪裡？

A. On a bus. 在巴士上。

B. In a boat. 在船上。

C. In a car. <u>在車子裡。</u>

* map〔mæp〕*n.* 地圖　　say〔se〕*v.* 寫著

　get off 離開　　exit〔'ɛgzɪt〕*n.*（高速公路）出口

　sign〔saɪn〕*n.*（交通）號誌

　Seattle〔si'ætl̩〕*n.* 西雅圖【位於美國華盛頓州的城市】

　mile〔maɪl〕*n.* 英里【距離單位，一英里為 1.6093 公里】

　shortcut〔'ʃɔrt,kʌt〕*n.* 捷徑　　***a bit of*** 少許

22. (**C**) W：Hey, Ricky.　How did you do on the exam?

女：嘿，瑞奇，你考試考得如何？

M：Don't ask.

男：別問了。

W：That bad, huh?

女：這麼糟，嗯？

Question：How did Ricky do on the exam?

瑞奇考試考得如何？

A. Very well. 非常好。　　　　B. So-so. 普普通通。

C. Not very well. <u>不太好。</u>

* do〔du〕*v.* 表現　　exam〔ɪg'zæm〕*n.* 考試（ = *examination* ）

huh〔hʌ〕*interj.* (用於發問或表示驚訝、異議) 嗯；啊

so-so〔'so,so〕*adv.* 馬馬虎虎；普普通通

23. (**C**) M：I'd like to buy a bracelet as a gift for my wife.　It's her birthday.

男：我想要買個手鐲給我老婆當作禮物，今天是她的生日。

W：Does your wife prefer silver, gold, or jade?

女：你老婆偏好銀的、金的、還是玉製的？

M：She likes silver.

男：她喜歡銀的。

Question：Where is this conversation taking place?

這對話發生在哪裡？

A. In a butcher shop. 在肉店。

B. In a bakery. 在麵包店。

C. In a jewelry store. <u>在珠寶店。</u>

* ***would like to*** + *V*. 想要～　　bracelet〔'breslɪt〕*n.* 手鐲

gift〔gɪft〕*n.* 禮物　　prefer〔prɪ'fɝ〕*v.* 偏好

silver〔'sɪlvɚ〕*n.* 銀；銀製品　　gold〔gold〕*n.* 黃金

jade〔dʒed〕*n.* 玉　　butcher〔'butʃɚ〕*n.* 屠夫；肉商

butcher shop 肉店　　bakery〔'bekərɪ〕*n.* 麵包店

jewelry〔'dʒuəlrɪ〕*n.* (統稱) 珠寶

24. (**C**) M : We're all headed down to the bowling alley after work.
Care to join us?

男：我們下班後要去保齡球館，要加入我們嗎？

W : I'd love to but I'm on a deadline. Maybe next time.

女：我想要去，但是今天是我工作完成期限，或許下一次吧。

M : Well, you know where to find us if you change your
mind.

男：嗯，如果妳改變心意，妳知道要去哪裡找我們。

Question : Why did the woman decline the man's invitation?
為什麼女士拒絕了男士的邀請？

A. She's not very fond of bowling. 她沒有很喜歡打保齡球。

B. She's going straight home after work.
她下班後要直接回家。

C. She's working on something urgent.
她正在做緊急的事情。

* ***be headed down to*** 前往　　bowling (ˈbolɪŋ) *n.* 保齡球
alley (ˈælɪ) *n.* 巷；道　　***bowling alley*** 保齡球場
after work 下班後　　***care to V.*** 想要
join (dʒɔɪn) *v.* 加入；和…一起做同樣的事
deadline (ˈdɛd͵laɪn) *n.* 截止日期；最後期限
change *one's* ***mind*** 改變心意　　decline (dɪˈklaɪn) *v.* 拒絕
invitation (͵ɪnvəˈteʃən) *n.* 邀請　　***be fond of*** 喜歡
straight (stret) *adv.* 直接地　　***work on*** 從事；致力於
urgent (ˈɝdʒənt) *adj.* 迫切的；緊急的

25. (**C**) M : You sure came home late last night, Lois. Why didn't
you call?

男：洛伊絲妳昨晚真的很晚才回家，為何不打個電話？

W : I'm sorry, Dad. We got lost on the way back from
Evansville.

女：爸爸，很抱歉，我們從埃文斯維爾回來的路上迷路了。

M：That's not what I asked you.

男：那不是我問你的問題。

Question：Why didn't Lois call last night?

　　　　爲什麼洛伊絲昨晚沒打電話？

A.　Her phone was dead.　她的手機不通。

B.　They got lost in Evansville.　她在埃文斯維爾迷路了。

C.　It is impossible to say.　<u>很難說。</u>

* sure〔ʃʊr〕*adv.* 的確；無疑地
　　Evansville〔'ɛvənzvɪl〕*n.* 埃文斯維爾【位於美國印第安那州的城市】
　　get lost 迷路　　　dead〔dɛd〕*adj.*（電話）斷的；不通的

26. (**C**)　W：Miles just called.　He said he's not coming today
　　　　　　because it's raining.

女：麥爾斯剛剛打電話來，他說他今天不會來，因爲在下雨。

M：Are you kidding?　He always says, "We can do this, or
　　we can do that…"

男：妳在開玩笑嗎？他總是說：「我們可以做這個，或是我們可
　　以做那個…」

W：Don't you know him?　He's all talk and no action.

女：你還不清楚他嗎？他光說不練。

Question：What does the woman say about Miles?

　　　　　關於麥爾斯，女士說了什麼？

A.　He changes his mind frequently.　他常常改變心意。

B.　He can be difficult to work with.　他會很難共事。

C.　He talks a lot but does little.　<u>他說很多但做得少。</u>

* kid〔kɪd〕*v.* 開玩笑　　　action〔'ækʃən〕*v.* 行動
　　all talk and no action 光說不做；空談
　　frequently〔'frikwəntlɪ〕*adv.* 經常
　　change one's ***mind*** 改變心意

27. (**B**) M：Hi, Luanne. I heard you had fun with Lenny at the carnival yesterday.

男：嗨，露安，我聽說妳昨天跟藍尼在嘉年華會玩得很愉快。

W：We did! Why didn't you come with us? It wasn't very crowded so it felt like we had the place to ourselves.

女：真的！你怎麼沒有一起來？沒有很擁擠，所以我們可以有自己的活動空間。

M：That's what Lenny said. But you know, I've been there so many times and I just wasn't up for it.

男：藍尼也是這麼說。但是妳知道的，我去過好幾次，就不太想去了。

Question：What does the man mean by saying he wasn't up for it? 男士說"he wasn't up for it"是什麼意思？

A. He didn't have enough money. 他沒足夠的錢。

B. He wasn't in the mood to go. 他不想去。

C. He doesn't like Lenny. 他不喜歡藍尼。

* ***have fun*** 玩得愉快　　carnival〔ˈkɑrnəvḷ〕*n.* 嘉年華會
crowded〔ˈkraʊdɪd〕*adj.* 擁擠的　　to〔tə , tu〕*prep.* 屬於
be up for 願意做～　　***be in the mood*** + ***to V.*** 有做…的心情

28. (**B**) W：Do you have this blouse in a size 3?

女：這件女用上衣你們有 3 號嗎？

M：I'm afraid we don't. That's the smallest size we have. But maybe one of our other locations has it in stock. Let me do some digging. I'll be back with you in a few minutes. Can you wait?

男：恐怕沒有，那是我們有的最小尺寸，但或許我們其他點的店有存貨。讓我查看看，我幾分鐘後會給您回覆，您能等一下嗎？

W：Sure! And thanks! I'll just continue browsing.

女：好的！謝謝！我會繼續隨意看看。

Question：What will the man most likely do next?

男士接下來最可能做什麼？

A. Change his clothes. 換衣服。

B. Make a phone call. 打電話。

C. Dig a hole. 挖個洞。

* blouse〔blaʊs〕*n.* 女用上衣

afraid〔ə'fred〕*adj.*（感到遺憾）恐怕…

location〔lo'keʃən〕*n.* 地點；位置

in stock 有存貨　　*do some + V-ing* 做點…

dig〔dɪg〕*v.* 探聽消息；挖（洞）

continue〔kən'tɪnju〕*v.* 繼續

browse〔braʊz〕*v.* 瀏覽；隨意看看

hole〔hol〕*n.* 洞

29.（ **A** ）M：Did you make reservations for dinner tonight?

男：妳今天的晚餐有訂位嗎？

W：Oh, I almost forgot! Thanks for reminding me.
　　I'll do it now.

女：噢，我差點忘了！謝謝你提醒我。我現在就去訂。

M：I hope it's not too late.

男：希望不會太晚。

Question：What are the speakers probably going to do
　　　　　 tonight? 說話者今天晚上可能要去哪裡？

A. Go out for dinner. 外出吃晚餐。

B. See a movie. 看電影。

C. Take a vacation. 度假。

* reservation〔͵rɛzɚ'veʃən〕 *n.* 預訂
  make reservations for 預定
  remind〔rɪ'maɪnd〕 *v.* 提醒；使想起
  go out 外出　***take a vacation*** 度假

30. (**C**) W : Hi John. So what seems to be the problem today?

女：嗨，約翰，今天看來有什麼問題嗎？

M : I got hit in the knee with a bat during baseball practice.

男：我膝蓋在練習棒球時被棒子擊中。

W : Ouch! Don't do that! [Laughs] OK, roll up your pant
leg and let me have a look.

女：哎唷！別那麼做呀！（笑）好吧，捲起你的褲管，讓我
看看。

Question : Who is the woman? 女士是什麼人？

A. She is a teacher. 她是個老師。

B. She is a baseball coach. 她是個棒球教練。

C. She is a doctor. 她是個醫生。

* seem〔sim〕 *v.* 似乎　　knee〔ni〕 *n.* 膝蓋
  hit〔hɪt〕 *v.* 打擊【三態為：hit-hit-hit】
  bat〔bæt〕 *n.* 棒子　　baseball〔'besͺbɔl〕 *n.* 棒球
  practice〔'præktɪs〕 *n.* 練習　　ouch〔autʃ〕 *interj.* 哎唷
  roll〔rol〕 *v.* 滾；捲　　pant〔pænt〕 *n.* 褲子
  leg〔lɛg〕 *n.*（衣服）腳的部分
  pant leg 褲管　　***have a look*** 看一看；瞧一瞧
  coach〔kotʃ〕 *n.* 教練

國中會考英文聽力 ⑥

一、辨識句意

　　本部分共 10 題，每題有三個圖片選項，請聽光碟放音機播出的題目，聽後從試題冊上 A、B、C 圖片中，選出一個最適合的回答。每題播出二遍。

例：　（聽）　John enjoys taking a bath.
　　　（看）

(A)　　　　　　　　　(B)　　　　　　　　　(C)

正確答案為 C，請在答案紙上塗黑作答。

1. 　　A. 　　　　　　B. 　　　　　　C.

2. 　　A. 　　　　　　B. 　　　　　　C.

 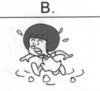 

3.　　A.　　　　B.　　　　C.

4.　　A.　　　　B.　　　　C.

5.　　A.　　　　B.　　　　C.

6.　　A.　　　　B.　　　　C.

7.　　A.　　　　B.　　　　C.

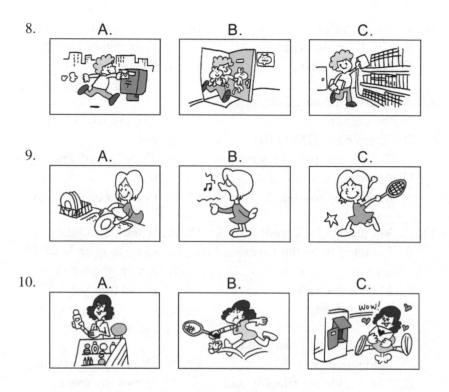

二、基本問答：選出最適合的回答，完成對話。

　　本部份共 10 題，每題光碟放音機會播出一個問句或直述句，聽後從試題冊上 A、B、C 三個選項中，選出一個最適合的回答。每題播出二遍。

　　例：　（聽） Hi, Mike. I haven't seen you for a long time.
　　　　　　　　 How are you doing?

　　　　　（看） A. I'm watching TV.
　　　　　　　　 B. I'm OK, thanks.
　　　　　　　　 C. I'm at school.

　　正確答案為 B，請在答案紙上塗黑作答。

11. A. No, I can't read.
　　B. No, I'd rather read a book.
　　C. No, but it shows.

12. A. There's a post office on the corner.
　　B. There's an ATM in the 7-Eleven across the street.
　　C. There are a lot of new faces in the neighborhood.

13. A. My alarm clock went off.
　　B. I wanted to be the first to arrive.
　　C. I had a doctor's appointment.

14. A. There is very snowy and cold weather.
　　B. The people are friendly and the scenery is beautiful.
　　C. They have many friends there.

15. A. Sure. Here you go.
　　B. There it is.
　　C. Thank you. I don't mind if I do.

16. A. Yes, we went to junior high school together.
　　B. Yes, she is.
　　C. Yes, I knew her.

17. A. Around five years ago.
　　B. They moved when I was 12.
　　C. For twenty-two years.

18. A. It shouldn't take more than an hour.
　　B. No, they haven't found him yet.
　　C. OK. I'll see you at the meeting.

19. A. Of course, everyone knows my name.
　　B. No. Everyone just calls me Lisa.
　　C. My brother calls my cell phone.

20. A. Yes, she does.
　　B. It sure was.
　　C. They always do.

三、言談理解（推論）

　　本部份共 10 題，每題光碟放音機會播出一段對話及一個相關的問題，聽後從試題冊上 A、B、C 三個選項中，選出一個最適合的回答。每題播出二遍。

例：　（聽）　(Man)　　　May I help you?

(Woman)　Yes, I'd like to look at that red sweater. How much is it?

(Man)　　　It's one thousand dollars.

Question:　Where are the man and the woman?

（看）　A.　In a restaurant.
B.　In the living room.
C.　In a department store.

正確答案為 C，請在答案紙上塗黑作答。

21. A. In a library.
B. In an emergency room.
C. In a hardware store.

22. A. She doesn't speak English.
B. She dreams of studying abroad.
C. She studied in the U.S.

23. A. He got fired.
B. He got promoted.
C. He got paid off.

24. A. Jenny is being coy.
B. Chad is jealous of Jenny.
C. Jenny has bad taste.

25. A. Boyfriend and girlfriend.
B. Cousins.
C. Brother and sister.

26. A. The man's dream.
B. The man's sleeping habits.
C. The man's weight problem.

27. A. He enjoys landscaping.
B. He is not good with plants.
C. He has a discolored thumb.

28. A. She has long legs.
B. She has fair skin.
C. She has blonde hair.

29. A. She likes it.
B. She hates it.
C. She wants it.

30. A. Graduate from college.
B. Attend art school.
C. Move home from Taipei.

國中會考英文聽力 ⑥ 詳解

一、辨識句意

1. (**C**) Tina is studying with Frank. 蒂娜和法蘭克一起唸書。

   * study〔'stʌdɪ〕*v.* 讀書；學習

2. (**B**) Robbie enjoys playing basketball. 羅比喜歡打籃球。

   * *enjoy + V-ing* 喜歡～　　basketball〔'bæskɪt,bɔl〕*n.* 籃球

3. (**C**) John is very helpful and considerate. 約翰會主動幫忙又體貼。

   * helpful〔'hɛlpfəl〕*adj.* 主動幫忙的
   considerate〔kən'sɪdərɪt〕*adj.* 體貼的

4. (**C**) Moira watches too much television. 莫拉看太多電視。

   * television〔'tɛlə,vɪʒən〕*n.* 電視

5. (**B**) Scott's favorite meal of the day is breakfast.
   史考特一天最愛的一餐是早餐。

   * favorite〔'fevrɪt〕*adj.* 最喜愛的　　meal〔mil〕*n.* 一餐

6. (**B**) Mr. Peebles is a wealthy stockbroker.
   皮布爾斯先生是位有錢的股票經紀人。

   * wealthy〔'wɛlθɪ〕*adj.* 富有的；有錢的
   stockbroker〔'stɑk,brokɚ〕*n.* 股票經紀人

7. (**A**) Mindy is learning to be a hairdresser.
   明迪正在學習當一位美髮師。

   * hairdresser〔'hɛr,drɛsɚ〕*n.* 美髮師；髮型設計師

8. (**C**) Paul is very studious. He spends a lot of time in the library.
   保羅很用功，他花很多時間在圖書館。

   * studious〔'stjudɪəs〕*adj.* 用功的　　library〔'laɪ,brɛrɪ〕*n.* 圖書館

9. (**A**) Mom is washing the dishes.　媽媽正在洗碗盤。

　　　* wash〔waʃ〕*v.* 洗
　　　　dish〔dɪʃ〕*n.* 碗盤（常說成 the dishes）

10. (**A**) Ms. Chen sells perfume in a department store.
　　　陳小姐在百貨公司賣香水。

　　　* Ms.〔mɪz〕*n.* …女士　　　perfume〔'pɝfjum〕*n.* 香水
　　　　department store 百貨公司

二、基本問答

11. (**B**) My favorite show is on tonight.　I can't wait.　Do you like
　　　to watch TV?
　　　我最喜歡的節目今晚會播出，我等不及了。你喜歡看電視嗎？

　　　A. No, I can't read.　不，我無法閱讀。
　　　B. No, I'd rather read a book.　<u>不，我寧可讀書。</u>
　　　C. No, but it shows.　不，但它出現了。

　　　* show〔ʃo〕*n.* 節目　*v.* 出現
　　　　can't wait 等不及　　　*would rather* + *V.* 寧可~

12. (**B**) Are you familiar with this neighborhood?　I'm looking for
　　　an ATM.　你對這附近熟嗎？我正在找自動提款機。

　　　A. There's a post office on the corner.　在轉角有一間郵局。
　　　B. There's an ATM in the 7-Eleven across the street.
　　　　<u>在對街的 7-11 裡有自動提款機。</u>
　　　C. There are a lot of new faces in the neighborhood.
　　　　在這鄰近地區有許多新面孔。

　　　* familiar〔fə'mɪljɚ〕*adj.* 熟悉的　*be familiar with* 對…熟悉
　　　　neighborhood〔'nebɚ,hʊd〕*n.* 鄰近地區
　　　　look for 尋找
　　　　ATM 自動櫃員機（= *automated-teller machine*）
　　　　post office 郵局　　　corner〔'kɔrnɚ〕*n.* 轉角處

13. (**C**) There you are, Stanley. Why are you late for class today?
史丹利，終於看到你了。為什麼你今天上課遲到？

    A. My alarm clock went off. 我的鬧鐘響了。

    B. I wanted to be the first to arrive. 我想要第一個到。

    C. I had a doctor's appointment. <u>我跟醫生有約。</u>

    * ***There you are.*** 你終於來了。【用於等待某人】
    be late for ～ ～遲到　　class〔klæs〕*n.* 上課（時間）
    alarm clock 鬧鐘　　***go off*** 響起　　arrive〔ə'raɪv〕*v.* 到達
    appointment〔ə'pɔɪtmənt〕*n.* 約定；預約

14. (**B**) Wow, you've been to Taiwan? What's it like?
哇，你去過台灣？那邊如何？

    A. There is very snowy and cold weather.
常常下雪而且天氣很冷。

    B. The people are friendly and the scenery is beautiful.
<u>人很友善，風景優美。</u>

    C. They have many friends there. 他們在那裡有很多朋友。

    * ***have been to*** ～ 曾經去過　　***What is ～ like?*** ～如何？
    snowy〔'snoɪ〕*adj.* 下雪的　　friendly〔'frɛndlɪ〕*adj.* 友善的
    scenery〔'sinərɪ〕*n.* 風景

15. (**C**) My French fries are delicious. Would you like to try one?
薯條很好吃，你要吃看看嗎？

    A. Sure. Here you go. 當然，拿去吧。

    B. There it is. 在那邊。

    C. Thank you. I don't mind if I do. 【詳見背景說明】
<u>謝謝，好的，那可太好了。</u>

    * ***French fries*** 炸薯條　　delicious〔dɪ'lɪʃəs〕*adj.* 好吃的；美味的
    Here you go. 你要的東西在這裡；拿去吧。
    mind〔maɪnd〕*v.* 介意
    I don't mind if I do. 那可太好了。【接受東西表示禮貌的方式】

16. (**A**) Have you met Rachel?　你見過瑞秋嗎？

　　A.　Yes, we went to junior high school together.
　　　　是的，我們一起上國中。
　　B.　Yes, she is.　是的，她是。
　　C.　Yes, I knew her.　是的，我知道她。

　　* meet〔mit〕v. 會見；認識　　**unior high school** 國中

17. (**C**) Tom's parents are getting divorced after 20 years together.
　　　　How long have your parents been married?
　　　　湯姆的雙親在結婚二十年後要離婚了。你父母結婚多久了？

　　A.　Around five years ago.　大概五年前。
　　B.　They moved when I was 12.　他們在我十二時歲搬家。
　　C.　For twenty-two years.　二十二年。

　　* divorce〔də'vɔrs〕v. 使離婚　　**get divorced** 離婚
　　　married〔'mærɪd〕adj. 結婚的；已婚的　　move〔muv〕v. 搬家

18. (**A**) Do you know how long the meeting will last?
　　　　你知道會議將會持續多久嗎？

　　A.　It shouldn't take more than an hour.
　　　　應該不會超過一小時。
　　B.　No, they haven't found him yet.　不，他們還沒找到他。
　　C.　OK.　I'll see you at the meeting.　好的，會議見。

　　* meeting〔'mitɪŋ〕n. 會議　　last〔læst〕v. 持續
　　　take〔tek〕v. 花費（時間）　　**not…yet** 尚未…

19. (**B**) My real name is Charles, but everyone calls me Chuck.　Do
　　　　you have a nickname?
　　　　我的真名是查爾斯，但是大家都叫我恰克。你有綽號嗎？

　　A.　Of course, everyone knows my name.
　　　　當然，每個人都知道我的名字。
　　B.　No.　Everyone just calls me Lisa.　不，大家就叫我麗莎。

C. My brother calls my cell phone. 我弟弟打我手機。

* nickname〔'nɪk͵nem〕*n.* 綽號　　***cell phone*** 手機

20. (**B**) Wasn't that game exciting? 那比賽不刺激嗎？

A. Yes, she does. 是的，她是。　 B. It sure was. <u>當然刺激。</u>

C. They always do. 他們總是這樣。

* game〔gem〕*n.* 比賽　　exciting〔ɪk'saɪtɪŋ〕*adj.* 刺激的
sure〔ʃʊr〕*adv.* 的確；無疑地

三、言談理解

21. (**B**) W：What happened to you?

女：你怎麼了？

M：I think I may have broken my ankle.　And you?

男：我想我的腳踝可能骨折了。妳呢？

W：Wow, that's terrible.　My injury is nothing compared to
　　yours.　I cut my hand on some broken glass.

女：哇，那真糟糕。我的傷不能跟你比，我手指被碎玻璃割傷了。

Question：Where is this conversation most likely taking
　　　　　place? 這對話最可能發生在哪裡？

A. In a library. 在圖書館裡。

B. In an emergency room. <u>在急診室裡。</u>

C. In a hardware store. 在五金行裡。

* ankle〔'æŋkḷ〕*n.* 腳踝　　terrible〔'tɛrəbḷ〕*adj.* 可怕的
compare〔kəm'pɛr〕*v.* 比較　　***nothing compared to*** 比不上
cut〔kʌt〕*v.* 割傷【三態為：cut-cut-cut】
broken〔'brokən〕*adj.* 破碎的　　glass〔glæs〕*n.* 玻璃
emergency〔ɪ'mɝdʒənsɪ〕*n.* 緊急狀況
emergency room 急診室
hardware〔'hɑrd͵wɛr〕*n.* (集合名詞) 五金器具
hardware store 五金行

22. (**C**) M : Gosh, Lucy. Your English is excellent. Have you
studied abroad?

　　男：天呀，露西，妳的英文很棒，妳有出國唸過書嗎？

　　W : I studied at a university in the U.S. for two years.

　　女：我在美國讀過兩年大學。

　　M : Wow! That's always been my dream. Where in the
U.S. did you live?

　　男：哇！那一直是我的夢想，妳住在美國哪裡？

　　Question : What is true about Lucy? 關於露西何者為真？

　　A. She doesn't speak English. 她不會說英文。

　　B. She dreams of studying abroad. 她夢想出國唸書。

　　C. She studied in the U.S. <u>她曾在美國唸書。</u>

　　* Gosh〔gɑʃ〕*interj.*（表示驚訝）唉呀！
　　excellent〔'ɛksl̩ənt〕*adj.* 極好的　　abroad〔ə'brɔd〕*adv.* 在國外
　　university〔͵junə'vɝsətɪ〕*n.* 大學
　　the U.S. 美國（= *the United States*）
　　dream〔drim〕*n. v.* 夢想　　***dream of*** 夢想…

23. (**B**) W : Congratulations, George! I heard you got a promotion
at work.

　　女：恭喜你，喬治！我聽說你工作升遷了。

　　M : Yes, I'm now an assistant manager. All that overtime
eventually paid off.

　　男：是的，我現在是副經理，加班終於有了成果。

　　W : So I bet that means a nice raise in salary to go along
with the new title?

　　女：那我敢說這就表示，伴隨著新職稱，你也加了不少薪吧？

　　Question : What happened to George? 喬治怎麼了？

　　A. He got fired. 他被開除了。

　　B. He got promoted. <u>他升遷了。</u>

　　C. He got paid off. 他被解雇了。

* congratulations (kən͵grætʃə'leʃənz) n. pl. 恭賀
  promotion (prə'moʃən) n. 升遷
  assistant (ə'sɪstənt) adj. 輔助的；副的
  manager ('mænɪdʒɚ) n. 經理　　*assistant manager* 副經理
  overtime ('ovɚ͵taɪm) n. 加班
  eventually (ɪ'vɛntʃʊəlɪ) adv. 終於　　*pay off* 得到回報
  bet (bɛt) v. 打賭；斷定　　raise (rez) n. 加薪
  salary ('sælərɪ) n. 薪水　　*go along with* 附帶；伴隨著
  title ('taɪtḷ) n. 頭銜　　fire (faɪr) v. 解雇
  promote (prə'mot) v. 使升遷　　*pay off* 付清工資解雇

24. (**A**) M : Hey, Jenny. How was your date with Chad last night?

　　　男：嘿，珍妮，妳昨晚跟查德的約會如何？

　　　W : Oh, it was OK. We went to see a concert.

　　　女：喔，很好。我們去看演唱會。

　　　M : And that's it? You're not going to share all the juicy
　　　　　details?

　　　男：就這樣？妳不打算分享有趣的細節？

　　　Question : What does the man imply? 男士暗示什麼？

　　　A. Jenny is being coy. 珍妮很害羞。

　　　B. Chad is jealous of Jenny. 查德嫉妒珍妮。

　　　C. Jenny has bad taste. 珍妮的品味很差。

　　　* date (det) n. 約會　　concert ('kɑnsɝt) n. 演唱會；音樂會
　　　That's it. 就這樣；就這些。　　share (ʃɛr) v. 分享
　　　juicy ('dʒusɪ) adj. (故事、謠言) 有趣的；生動的
　　　detail ('ditel) n. 細節　　imply (ɪm'plaɪ) v. 暗示
　　　coy (kɔɪ) adj. 害羞的；嬌羞的
　　　jealous ('dʒɛləs) adj. 嫉妒的　　***be jealous of*** 嫉妒
　　　taste (test) n. 品味

25. (**A**) W : Who was that I saw you hugging in the cafeteria this
　　　　　morning?

　　　女：今早我看到你在自助餐廳擁抱的人是誰？

M : That was my cousin Ella.　She just transferred to this
　　school.　I'll introduce you to her.

男：那是我的姪女艾拉，她剛轉學到這邊。我會介紹給妳認識。

W : Oh, I'm sorry.　I thought you were two-timing me
　　behind my back.

女：噢，很抱歉。我以為你在我背後劈腿。

Question : What is the relationship between the speakers?
　　　　　說話者的關係是什麼？

A.　Boyfriend and girlfriend.　男女朋友。

B.　Cousins.　表兄妹。

C.　Brother and sister.　兄妹。

* hug〔hʌg〕*v.* 擁抱　　cafeteria〔͵kæfə'tɪrɪə〕*n.* 自助餐廳
　cousin〔'kʌzn̩〕*n.*（表）堂兄弟姊妹
　transfer〔træns'fɝ〕*v.* 轉學
　introduce〔͵ɪntrə'djus〕*v.* 介紹
　two-time〔'tu͵taɪm〕*v.*（背著愛人）欺騙；劈腿
　relationship〔rɪ'leʃən͵ʃɪp〕*n.* 關係

26. (**A**) M : I had the strangest dream last night.　Eric was a cat and
　　　　　　　I was a mouse, and he was chasing me around this big
　　　　　　　old house.

男：我昨天做了一個很怪的夢。艾瑞克是隻貓，而我是老鼠，
　　然後他追著我在這大大的舊屋子裡跑。

W : I think you need to stop having the midnight snacks.
　　It's clearly affecting your sleep.

女：我想你需要停止吃宵夜，這顯然影響了你的睡眠。

M : Really?　Do you think so?　It seems to me like all
　　dreams are weird.　Some just more than others.

男：真的嗎？妳這樣覺得？似乎對我而言，所有的夢都很怪，
　　只是有些比其他的更怪。

Question : What are the speakers discussing?
　　　　　說話者在討論什麼？

A. The man's dream. 男子的夢。
B. The man's sleeping habits. 男子的睡眠習慣。
C. The man's weight problem. 男子的體重問題。

* mouse〔maʊs〕*n.* 老鼠　　chase〔tʃes〕*v.* 追逐
midnight〔'mɪd,naɪt〕*n.* 午夜　　snack〔snæk〕*n.* 點心；宵夜
clearly〔'klɪrlɪ〕*adv.* 顯然地；明顯地
affect〔ə'fɛkt〕*v.* 影響　　seem〔sim〕*v.* 似乎
weird〔wɪrd〕*adj.* 怪異的　　habit〔hæbɪt〕*n.* 習慣
weight〔wet〕*n.* 體重

27. (**B**) W : I need someone to look after my plants while I'm out
　　　　　　of town next week.
　　　女：我下週到外地的時候，需要有人照顧我的植物。
　　　M : Don't look at me. I'm no green thumb.
　　　男：別看我，我不擅長照顧植物。
　　　W : All you need to do is water them and talk to them a
　　　　　　little bit. A trained seal could do it.
　　　女：你要做的就只是澆水和跟它們講些話。受過訓練的海豹都
　　　　　　會做。
　　　Question : What does the man imply? 男士暗示什麼？
　　　A. He enjoys landscaping. 他喜歡景觀美化的工作。
　　　B. He is not good with plants. 他不太會照顧植物。
　　　C. He has a discolored thumb. 他的拇指被染色了。

* ***look after*** 照顧　　plant〔plænt〕*n.* 植物
town〔taʊn〕*n.* 城鎮　　***out of town*** 出城；到外地
thumb〔θʌm〕*n.* 拇指
green thumb 栽培植物的才能；精通園藝
all one need to do is + V. 某人所需要做的就是～
water〔'wɔtɚ〕*v.* 給…澆水　　***a little bit*** 一點；少許
seal〔sil〕*n.* 海豹　　***enjoy + V-ing*** 喜愛～
landscape〔'lænskep〕*v.* 景觀美化（或園藝）工作
be good with 善於（處理）
discolor〔dɪs'kʌlɚ〕*v.* 使…變色

28. (**C**) M：What do you think of Rita? Isn't she pretty?

男：妳覺得瑞塔如何？她不美嗎？

W：Hmm. I thought you didn't like blondes.

女：嗯，我覺得你不喜歡金髮的女人。

M：I usually don't, but Rita is the exception.

男：我通常不喜歡，但我覺得瑞塔是例外。

Question：What is true about Rita? 關於瑞塔何者為真？

A. She has long legs. 她的腿很長。

B. She has fair skin. 她的皮膚很白。

C. She has blonde hair. 她有金髮。

* ***What do you think of~?*** 你覺得~如何？

pretty〔'prɪtɪ〕*adj.* 漂亮的

blonde〔blɑnd〕*n.* 金髮的（女）人　*adj.* 金髮的

exception〔ɪk'sɛpʃən〕*n.* 例外

fair〔fɛr〕*adj.*（皮膚）白晰的

29. (**A**) W：Mother's Day is next week. Have you gotten anything for Mom yet?

女：下週是母親節，你有買了什麼要給媽了嗎？

M：No, I haven't had a chance. Would you like to go in on something for her, like maybe flowers?

男：還沒，一直沒有機會去。妳想要一起買東西送她，像是花？

W：That's a good idea. We can pool our resources, and she does love roses.

女：那是個好主意，我們可以集資，而且她真的很喜歡玫瑰。

Question：What does the woman think about the man's idea? 女士覺得男士的主意如何？

A. She likes it. 她喜歡。

B. She hates it. 她討厭。

C. She wants it. 她想要。

* ***Mother's Day*** 母親節　　get〔gɛt〕*v.* 買

yet〔jɛt〕*adv.* 已經　　chance〔tʃæns〕*n.* 機會

***go in on* sth.** 共同分擔（費用）　　**pool**〔pul〕*v.* 共同出（資）
resource〔rɪ'sors〕*n.* 財力；資源
***do / does* + V.** 真的～；的確～　　**rose**〔roz〕*n.* 玫瑰
hate〔het〕*v.* 討厭

30. (**B**) M : Laura has decided to move to Taipei next year. She got accepted to an art school there.

男：蘿拉決定明年要搬到台北，她已獲准進入那裡的一間藝術學校就讀。

W : Where will she stay? Taipei is a huge city. I can't imagine Laura living by herself like that.

女：她要住哪？台北是個大都市，我無法想像蘿拉自己一個人住。

M : No, you're right about that. She will stay with her aunt in the Wanhua District.

男：是的，妳說的對。她會跟她阿姨一起住在萬華區。

Question : What will Laura do next year?

　　　蘿拉打算明年做什麼？

A. Graduate from college. 從大學畢業。

B. Attend art school. <u>就讀藝術學校。</u>

C. Move home from Taipei. 搬家離開台北。

* **decide**〔dɪ'saɪd〕*v.* 決定　　**move**〔muv〕*v.* 搬家
accept〔ək'sɛpt〕*v.* 接受　　**art**〔ɑrt〕*n.* 藝術
stay〔ste〕*v.* 暫住　　**huge**〔hjudʒ〕*adj.* 巨大的
imagine〔ɪ'mædʒɪn〕*v.* 想像
aunt〔ænt〕*n.* 阿姨；姑媽
district〔'dɪstrɪkt〕*n.* （行政）區
graduate〔'grædʒʊˌet〕*v.* 畢業
college〔'kɑlɪdʒ〕*n.* 大學　　**attend**〔ə'tɛnd〕*v.* 上（學）
move home 搬家

國中會考英文聽力 ⑦

一、辨識句意

本部分共 10 題，每題有三個圖片選項，請聽光碟放音機播出的題目，聽後從試題冊上 A、B、C 圖片中，選出一個最適合的回答。每題播出二遍。

例： （聽） John enjoys taking a bath.
　　 （看）

(A)  (B)  (C)

正確答案為 C，請在答案紙上塗黑作答。

1. A. 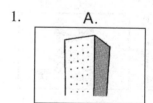 B.  C.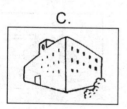

2. A.  B. 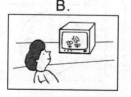 C.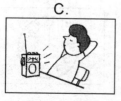

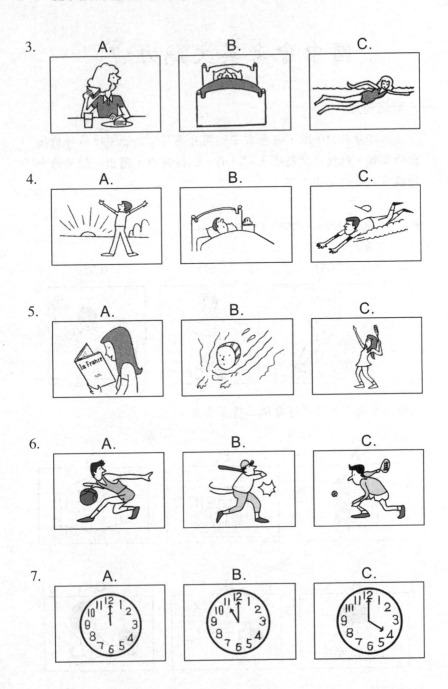

8. A.   B.   C.

9. A.   B.   C.

10. A.   B.   C.

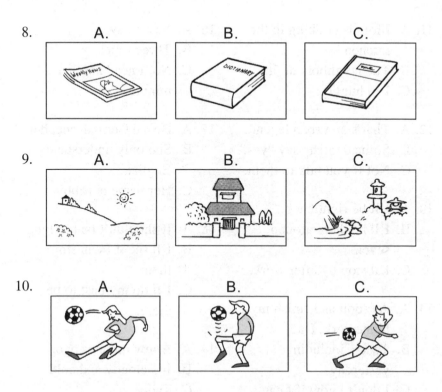

二、基本問答：選出最適合的回答，完成對話。

本部份共 10 題，每題光碟放音機會播出一個問句或直述句，聽後從試題冊上 A、B、C 三個選項中，選出一個最適合的回答。每題播出二遍。

例： （聽） Hi, Mike. I haven't seen you for a long time. How are you doing?

（看） A. I'm watching TV.
B. I'm OK, thanks.
C. I'm at school.

正確答案爲 B，請在答案紙上塗黑作答。

11. A. Mom is cooking in the kitchen.
    B. The neighbors do it.
    C. I'm hungry.

12. A. That's an urban legend.
    B. Some dentists say "yes."
    C. Not if you talk to them.

13. A. I'll be right back.
    B. I'll be there around seven.
    C. I'll stop by after work.

14. A. As soon as I finish my homework, Dad.
    B. Twice, including yesterday.
    C. I don't know if I can make it, Mr. Grant.

15. A. Weekdays from 2:00 – 3:00 pm.
    B. It's in the Humanities building.
    C. He doesn't have it.

16. A. Yes, I have.
    B. Three times.
    C. No, I need another minute.

17. A. He's a German shepherd.
    B. She only understands English.
    C. Her name is Libby.

18. A. It shouldn't be too long.
    B. I'll see if I can stop them.
    C. I'll do my best to be there.

19. A. A few minutes ago.
    B. It's cloudy and cold.
    C. Twice.

20. A. I thought you had some already.
    B. It's right there.
    C. I'll be ready to leave soon.

三、言談理解（推論）

　　本部份共 10 題，每題光碟放音機會播出一段對話及一個相關的問題，聽後從試題冊上 A、B、C 三個選項中，選出一個最適合的回答。每題播出二遍。

例： （聽）(Man)　　May I help you?
　　　　　(Woman)　Yes, I'd like to look at that red sweater.
　　　　　　　　　　How much is it?
　　　　　(Man)　　It's one thousand dollars.

　　　　　Question:　Where are the man and the woman?

（看）A. In a restaurant.
　　　B. In the living room.
　　　C. In a department store.

正確答案為 C，請在答案紙上塗黑作答。

21. A. That she speaks Japanese.
　　B. That she likes Japanese food.
　　C. That she is Japanese.

22. A. On the street.
　　B. In an airport.
　　C. At a party.

23. A. There is toothpaste on his face.
　　B. The woman is staring at him.
　　C. His socks don't match.

24. A. A public telephone.
　　B. Her cell phone.
　　C. The restroom.

25. A. A high price.
　　B. A long time.
　　C. A bad deal.

26. A. To the market.
　　B. To the bank.
　　C. To the café.

27. A. He likes to spread rumors.
　　B. He is very upset.
　　C. He dumped his girlfriend.

28. A. The man must be lazy.
　　B. The man must be in pain.
　　C. The man must be generous.

29. A. The black shirt is too tight.
　　B. The woman is fat.
　　C. He could lose some weight.

30. A. At home.
　　B. In Paris.
　　C. In Egypt.

國中會考英文聽力 ⑦ 詳解

一、辨識句意

1. (**B**) My house is in a quiet neighborhood.
   我的房子在一個安靜的地區。
   * quiet 〔'kwaɪət 〕 adj. 安靜的
     neighborhood 〔'nebə,hud 〕 n. 鄰近地區

2. (**C**) Greg enjoys listening to the radio. 葛瑞格喜歡聽廣播。
   * *enjoy + V-ing* 喜歡～   *listen to* 聽
     radio 〔'redɪ,o 〕 n. 廣播

3. (**A**) Ms. Swanson is having lunch. 史旺森小姐正在吃午餐。
   * have 〔 hæv 〕 v. 吃；喝   lunch 〔 lʌntʃ 〕 n. 午餐

4. (**B**) Oliver sleeps late on the weekends. 奧利佛週末睡很晚。
   * late 〔 let 〕 adv. 晚   weekend 〔'wik'ɛnd 〕 n. 週末

5. (**C**) Irene is a talented tennis player. 艾琳是個有天分的網球選手。
   * talented 〔'tæləntɪd 〕 adj. 有天分的
     tennis 〔'tɛnɪs 〕 n. 網球   player 〔'pleə 〕 n. 選手

6. (**B**) Joe is captain of the baseball team. 喬是棒球隊隊長。
   * captain 〔'kæptən 〕 n. (球隊的) 隊長
     baseball 〔'bes,bɔl 〕 n. 棒球   team 〔 tim 〕 n. 隊

7. (**C**) It's four in the afternoon. 現在是下午四點。
   * afternoon 〔,æftə'nun 〕 n. 下午

8. (**B**) I can't find that word in the dictionary.
   我在字典裡找不到那個字。
   * word 〔 wɜd 〕 n. 字；單字
     dictionary 〔'dɪkʃən,ɛrɪ 〕 n. 字典

9. (**A**) It's very relaxing to spend the day in the countryside.
　　　　在鄉下度過一天是很輕鬆愉快的。

　　　* relaxing〔rɪ'læksɪŋ〕*adj.* 令人放鬆的；輕鬆愉快的
　　　spend〔spɛnd〕*v.* 度過（時間、假期）
　　　countryside〔'kʌntrɪˌsaɪd〕*n.* 鄉村地區

10. (**B**) Look at Terry! He's bouncing the ball on his knee.
　　　　看看泰瑞！他在用膝蓋踢球。

　　　* bounce〔baʊns〕*v.* 使反彈；使彈回
　　　knee〔ni〕*n.* 膝蓋

二、基本問答

11. (**A**) What's that smell? Is something burning?
　　　　那是什麼氣味？有東西在燒嗎？

　　　A. Mom is cooking in the kitchen. <u>媽媽在廚房煮東西。</u>
　　　B. The neighbors do it. 鄰居做的。
　　　C. I'm hungry. 我很餓。

　　　* smell〔smɛl〕*n.* 氣味　　burn〔bɝn〕*v.* 燃燒
　　　kitchen〔'kɪtʃɪn〕*n.* 廚房　　neighbor〔'nebɚ〕*n.* 鄰居

12. (**A**) Did you know that cell phones cause brain damage?
　　　　你知道手機對腦部有害嗎？

　　　A. That's an urban legend. <u>那是個都市傳說。</u>
　　　B. Some dentists say "yes." 有些牙醫說「是的」。
　　　C. Not if you talk to them. 如果你不跟它們講話就不會。

　　　* ***cell phone*** 手機　　cause〔kɔz〕*v.* 造成
　　　brain〔bren〕*n.* 腦　　damage〔'dæmɪdʒ〕*n.* 損傷；傷害
　　　urban〔'ɝbən〕*adj.* 都市的　　legend〔'lɛdʒənd〕*n.* 傳說
　　　urban legend 都市傳說【（往往含有幽默、恐怖或教訓成分的）來
　　　　源不明、缺少或無證據，但自然地以各種形式出現的當代故事或傳說】
　　　dentist〔'dɛntɪst〕*n.* 牙醫

13. (**A**) Hey! Where are you going? 嘿！你要去哪裡？

    A. I'll be right back. 我馬上回來。

    B. I'll be there around seven. 我大概七點會到那邊。

    C. I'll stop by after work. 我下班後會順道拜訪。

    * right〔raɪt〕*adv.* 立刻；馬上　　***stop by*** 順道拜訪
    after work 下班後

14. (**A**) It's getting late, Kim. When will you take a break and eat your dinner?

    時間很晚了，金。你何時要休息一下吃晚餐呢？

    A. As soon as I finish my homework, Dad.
      我一做完功課就去，爸爸。

    B. Twice, including yesterday. 兩次，包含昨天。

    C. I don't know if I can make it, Mr. Grant.
      我不知道我做不做得到，葛蘭特先生。

    * break〔brek〕*n.* 休息時間　　***take a break*** 休息一下
    as soon as 一…就　　finish〔'fɪnɪʃ〕*v.* 完成
    including〔ɪn'kludɪŋ〕*prep.* 包括　　***make it*** 成功；辦到

15. (**A**) I need to speak with Professor Jones. Do you know his office hours?

    我需要跟瓊斯教授談談，你知道他的上班時間嗎？

    A. Weekdays from 2:00 – 3:00 pm.
      平日下午兩點到三點。

    B. It's in the Humanities building. 在人文大樓。

    C. He doesn't have it. 他沒有。

    * professor〔prə'fɛsɚ〕*n.* 教授
    office hours 辦公時間；上班時間
    weekday〔'wik,de〕*n.* 平日　　***p.m.*** 下午（ = *post meridiem* ）
    humanities〔hju'mænətɪz〕*n. pl.* 人文；人文學科
    building〔'bɪldɪŋ〕*n.* 建築物；大樓

16. (**C**) Welcome to the Pizza Palace. Are you ready to order?
　　　　歡迎來到披薩皇宮，準備好要點餐了嗎？

　　　A.　Yes, I have.
　　　　　是的，我點過了。
　　　B.　Three times. 三次。
　　　C.　No, I need another minute.
　　　　　<u>不，我還需要一點時間。</u>

　　　* pizza〔'pitsə〕n. 披薩　　palace〔'pælɪs〕n. 宮殿
　　　　order〔'ɔrdɚ〕v. 點（菜）　　time〔taɪm〕n. 次數
　　　　minute〔'mɪnɪt〕n. 一會兒；片刻

17. (**C**) Oh, what a lovely kitten! What's her name?
　　　　喔，好可愛的小貓！牠叫什麼名字？

　　　A.　He's a German shepherd. 牠是德國牧羊犬。
　　　B.　She only understands English. 牠只懂英文。
　　　C.　Her name is Libby. <u>牠的名字是利比。</u>

　　　* lovely〔'lʌvlɪ〕adj. 可愛的　　kitten〔'kɪtn̩〕n. 小貓
　　　　German〔'dʒɝmən〕adj. 德國的
　　　　shepherd〔'ʃɛpɚd〕n. 牧羊人
　　　　German shepherd 德國牧羊犬

18. (**C**) I hope you can make it to my birthday party, Louis.
　　　　我希望你可以來我的生日派對，路易斯。

　　　A.　It shouldn't be too long. 應該不會太久。
　　　B.　I'll see if I can stop them.
　　　　　我看看能不能阻止他們。
　　　C.　I'll do my best to be there. <u>我會盡可能到。</u>

　　　* *make it to* 出席；到場　　stop〔stɑp〕v. 阻止
　　　　do one's best 盡力

19. (**B**) What's the weather like outside? 外面天氣如何？

    A. A few minutes ago. 幾分鐘前。

    B. It's cloudy and cold. 多雲而且寒冷。

    C. Twice. 兩次。

    * ***What is ~ like?*** ～如何？
    outside〔'aut'saɪd〕*adv.* 在外面
    cloudy〔'klaudɪ〕*adj.* 多雲的   twice〔twaɪs〕*adv.* 兩次

20. (**A**) I can't believe you ate the last piece of cake and didn't leave any for me!

    我無法相信你把最後一片蛋糕吃了，一片都沒留給我！

    A. I thought you had some already.

        我以為你已經吃了一些。

    B. It's right there. 就在那邊。

    C. I'll be ready to leave soon. 我準備好馬上要走了。

    * believe〔bə'liv〕*v.* 相信
    piece〔pis〕*n.* 一片（用於不可數名詞）
    leave〔liv〕*v.* 留下   have〔hæv〕*v.* 吃；喝

三、言談理解

21. (**A**) M：How long have you lived in Japan?

    男：妳在日本住多久了？

    W：For over 20 years.

    女：超過二十年。

    M：Really? Your Japanese must be excellent by now.

    男：真的嗎？那妳的日文現在一定超好。

    Question：What does the man assume about the woman?

        男士認為女士如何？

A. That she speaks Japanese. 她會說日文。

B. That she likes Japanese food. 她喜歡日本食物。

C. That she is Japanese. 她是日本人。

* Japan〔dʒə'pæn〕*n.* 日本　　Japanese〔͵dʒæpə'niz〕*n.* 日語
excellent〔'ɛksḷ̩ənt〕*adj.* 很好的；很棒的
assume〔ə'sum〕*v.* 認為；假定

22. (**C**) W : Haven't we met somewhere before? You look so
familiar to me.

　　女：我們之前是不是在哪裡見過？你看起來很面熟。

　　M : I was just thinking the same thing. Were you at Tom
Edwards' retirement party?

　　男：我也是這麼想，妳是不是有去湯姆愛德華茲的退休派對？

　　W : Yes! I remember now.

　　女：是的！現在我想起來了。

　　Question : Where did the speakers meet?

　　　　　　　說話者在哪裡見過面？

A. On the street. 在街上。

B. In an airport. 在機場裡。

C. At a party. 在派對上。

* familiar〔fə'mɪljɚ〕*adj.* 熟悉的；面熟的
be familiar to *sb.* 對某人來說很面熟
retirement〔rɪ'taɪrmənt〕*n.* 退休
party〔'pɑrtɪ〕*n.* 派對；聚會　　airport〔'ɛr͵port〕*n.* 機場

23. (**A**) M : What's wrong? Why are you looking at me like that?

　　男：怎麼了？妳為何那樣看我？

　　W : There's dried toothpaste all around your mouth.

　　女：你嘴巴周圍有乾掉的牙膏。

M : Oh, how embarrassing!

男：喔，真尷尬！

Question : Why is the man embarrassed?

為何男士感到尷尬？

A. There is toothpaste on his face. 他臉上有牙膏。

B. The woman is staring at him. 女士正在瞪他。

C. His socks don't match. 他襪子不成對。

* ***What's wrong?*** 怎麼了？　　　dried〔draɪd〕*adj.* 乾的
　toothpaste〔'tuθ,pest〕*n.* 牙膏
　embarrassing〔ɪm'bærəsɪŋ〕*adj.* 令人尷尬的
　stare〔ster〕*v.* 凝視；瞪著　　***stare at*** 凝視；瞪著
　match〔mætʃ〕*v.* 一致；配合

24. (**A**) W : Excuse me, is there a public telephone nearby? My
　　　　　　cell phone is dead and it's extremely urgent.

女：抱歉，這附近有公共電話嗎？我的手機沒電了，現在很緊急。

M : Here, you can use my cell phone.

男：拿去，妳可以用我的手機。

W : Thanks a lot.

女：非常感謝。

Question : What is the woman looking for? 女士在找什麼？

A. A public telephone. 公共電話。

B. Her cell phone. 她的手機。

C. The restroom. 廁所。

* public〔'pʌblɪk〕*adj.* 公共的　　nearby〔'nɪr,baɪ〕*adv.* 在附近
　cell phone 手機　　dead〔dɛd〕*adj.* 沒電的
　extremely〔ɪk'strimlɪ〕*adv.* 極度地；非常
　urgent〔'ɝdʒənt〕*adj.* 緊急的；迫切的
　look for 尋找　　restroom〔'rɛst,rum〕*n.* 洗手間；廁所

25. (**A**) M：That's a nice bicycle. It must have cost an arm and
a leg.

男：那腳踏車真棒，一定花了不少錢。

W：Not really. I got it on sale. Fifty percent off!

女：其實沒有，我特價時買的，五折！

M：Wow, that's quite a deal!

男：哇，真划算！

Question：What does the man mean by "an arm and a leg"?

男子說 "an arm and a leg" 是什麼意思？

A. A high price. 價格很高。

B. A long time. 很長一段時間。

C. A bad deal. 不好的交易。

* ***cost an arm and a leg*** 所費不貲；花很大的代價
(= *be very expensive*)

not really 不完全是；不見得   ***on sale*** 特價；廉價出售
deal〔dil〕*n.* 交易   ***quite a deal*** 很划算 (= *a good deal*)
price〔praɪs〕*n.* 價格

26. (**C**) W：Hey, are you going down to the café?

女：嘿，你正要去咖啡店嗎？

M：Yes. Would you like me to get you something?

男：是的，妳要我幫妳買什麼嗎？

W：That would be great! How about a coffee and a
doughnut?

女：那真是太好了！買杯咖啡和甜甜圈如何？

Question：Where is the man going? 男士要去哪裡？

A. To the market. 去市場。   B. To the bank. 去銀行。

C. To the café. 去咖啡店。

* *go down to*　去；到　　café〔kə'fe〕 *n.* 咖啡店
　　　　great〔gret〕 *adj.* 很棒的　　 *How about~?*　～如何？
　　　　doughnut〔'donət〕 *n.* 甜甜圈
　　　　market〔'markɪt〕 *n.* 市場　　bank〔bæŋk〕 *n.* 銀行

27. (**B**) M：What's wrong with Peter this morning? He's really
　　　　　　　　upset.

　　　　　男：彼得今天早上怎麼了？他真的很沮喪。

　　　　　W：I don't want to spread any rumors, but I heard Helen
　　　　　　　dumped him yesterday.

　　　　　女：我不想要散播謠言，但我聽說海倫甩了他。

　　　　　M：Well, they've definitely been having problems, so it
　　　　　　　wouldn't surprise me. Poor guy. He really liked
　　　　　　　Helen, too.

　　　　　男：嗯，他們的確一直有些問題，所以我並不感到驚訝。真可憐，
　　　　　　　他真的很喜歡海倫。

　　　　　Question：What do we know about Peter?

　　　　　　　　　　我們可以知道彼得怎麼了？

　　　　　A. He likes to spread rumors.　他喜歡散播謠言。

　　　　　B. He is very upset.　他很沮喪。

　　　　　C. He dumped his girlfriend.　他甩了他的女朋友。

　　　　　* *What's wrong with* sb*.?*　某人怎麼了？
　　　　　upset〔ʌp'sɛt〕 *adj.* 沮喪的；不高興的
　　　　　spread〔sprɛd〕 *v.* 散播；散佈
　　　　　rumor〔'rumɚ〕 *n.* 謠言　　dump〔dʌmp〕 *v.* 拋棄
　　　　　definitely〔'dɛfənɪtlɪ〕 *adv.* 確實地
　　　　　surprise〔sə'praɪz〕 *v.* 使驚訝　　guy〔gaɪ〕 *n.* 人；傢伙

28. (**B**) W：What happened to your face? It looks swollen.

　　　　　女：你的臉怎麼了？看起來很腫。

M : I had to get a tooth pulled today.

男：我今天去拔牙。

W : Did the dentist give you any medication for the pain?

女：醫生有給你止痛的藥嗎？

Question : What does the woman think?　女士有什麼想法？

A. The man must be lazy.　男士一定很懶惰。

B. The man must be in pain.　男士一定感覺很痛。

C. The man must be generous.　男士一定很慷慨。

* swollen〔'swolən〕*adj.* 腫的　　pull〔pυl〕*v.* 拉出；拔出
  dentist〔'dɛntɪst〕*n.* 牙醫
  medication〔,mɛdɪ'keʃən〕*n.* 藥物
  pain〔pen〕*n.* 疼痛
  lazy〔'lezɪ〕*adj.* 懶惰的　　***be in pain*** 痛苦
  generous〔'dʒɛnərəs〕*adj.* 慷慨的

29. (**C**) M : Which shirt looks better on me, the black one or the
　　　　　　　gray one?

男：哪件襯衫我穿起來比較好看，黑色還是灰色？

W : The black one, I think. It fits you better. The gray
　　one is a little too tight.

女：黑色的，我覺得。比較適合你，灰色的有點太緊了。

M : You're right. Maybe if I dropped a few pounds I
　　could wear the gray one.

男：妳說得對，或許我再瘦個幾磅就可以穿灰色的。

Question : What does the man imply?　男士暗示什麼？

A. The black shirt is too tight.　黑色襯衫太緊。

B. The woman is fat.　女士太胖。

C. He could lose some weight.　他可以減些體重。

* shirt〔ʃɝt〕n. 襯衫　　gray〔gre〕adj. 灰色的
  look good on sb. （衣服）適合某人
  fit〔fɪt〕v. 適合　　tight〔taɪt〕adj. 緊的
  drop〔drɑp〕v. 減少
  pound〔paʊnd〕n. 磅【重量單位，一磅爲 0.45 公斤】
  weight〔wet〕n. 重量　　**lose weight** 減重

30.（**B**） W：I can't wait for my vacation this summer.

女：我等不及我夏天的假期了。

M：Are you going to take a trip abroad?

男：妳打算出國旅遊嗎？

W：Yes. I'd like to visit Egypt but Danny has his heart
　　set on Paris.

女：是的，我想去埃及，但是丹尼一心想要去巴黎。

Question：Where will the woman most likely spend her
　　　　　summer vacation?

　　　　　女士最可能去哪裡度過暑假？

　A. At home. 在家。

　B. In Paris. 在巴黎。

　C. In Egypt. 在埃及。

* **can't wait for** 等不及～
  vacation〔və'keʃən〕n. 假期
  trip〔trɪp〕n. 旅行　　**take a trip** 去旅行
  abroad〔ə'brɔd〕adv. 到國外　　**would like to** + **V.** 想要～
  Egypt〔'idʒəpt〕n. 埃及【位於非洲北部的國家】
  have one's heart set on 一心想要～
  Paris〔'pærɪs〕n. 巴黎【法國首都】　　spend〔spɛnd〕v. 度過
  summer vacation 暑假

國中會考英文聽力⑧

一、辨識句意

本部分共 10 題，每題有三個圖片選項，請聽光碟放音機播出的題目，聽後從試題冊上 A、B、C 圖片中，選出一個最適合的回答。每題播出二遍。

例： （聽） John enjoys taking a bath.
　　 （看）

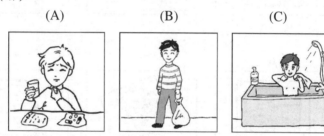

（A）　　　　　　　（B）　　　　　　　（C）

正確答案為 C，請在答案紙上塗黑作答。

1.

2.

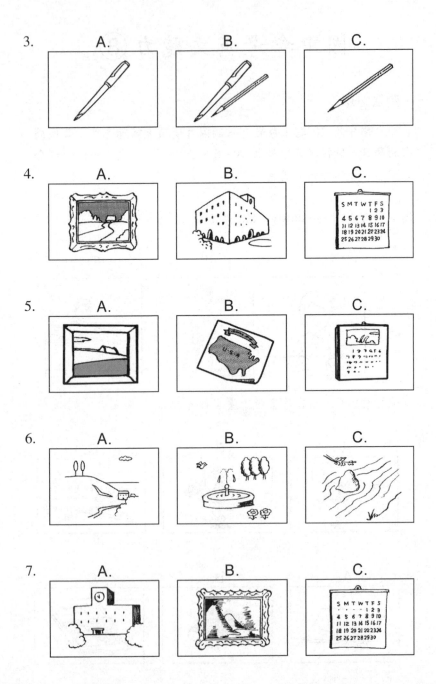

8.　　A.　　　　　B.　　　　　C.

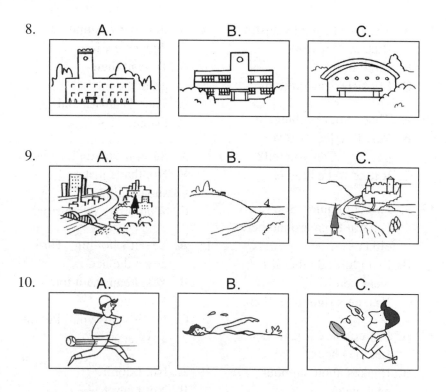

9.　　A.　　　　　B.　　　　　C.

10.　　A.　　　　　B.　　　　　C.

二、基本問答：選出最適合的回答，完成對話。

本部份共 10 題，每題光碟放音機會播出一個問句或直述句，聽後從試題冊上 A、B、C 三個選項中，選出一個最適合的回答。每題播出二遍。

例：　（聽）　Hi, Mike. I haven't seen you for a long time.
　　　　　　　How are you doing?

　　　（看）　A. I'm watching TV.
　　　　　　　B. I'm OK, thanks.
　　　　　　　C. I'm at school.

正確答案為 B，請在答案紙上塗黑作答。

11. A. The latest song by Justin
　　　Bieber, "Move It."
　　B. I like it, too.
　　C. My sister gave it to me.

12. A. That's your problem.
　　B. Yes, I've lost twelve
　　　pounds. Can you tell?
　　C. It used to be blonde.

13. A. I wish I could. Sorry,
　　　I'm not from around here
　　　either.
　　B. I wouldn't do that if I
　　　were you.
　　C. Yes, he's right over there.

14. A. I'm not sure if it works.
　　　Let me check.
　　B. It takes about an hour
　　　each way.
　　C. Not bad. I'm still getting
　　　used to it.

15. A. That ship has sailed.
　　B. No. I'm not interested.
　　C. You can't believe
　　　everything you see and
　　　hear.

16. A. It's always sunny in
　　　Sunshine City.
　　B. To visit their
　　　grandparents.
　　C. There's Olivia and
　　　Daniel.

17. A. Sure, if you do it right.
　　B. No, that's just a
　　　superstition.
　　C. Who broke the mirror?

18. A. Yes, it's boiling. Turn
　　　down the heat.
　　B. Yes, I can see it too.
　　　Your turn.
　　C. No, it's just you. Put on
　　　a sweater.

19. A. No, I don't.
　　B. No, I can't.
　　C. No, I will.

20. A. I have swim lessons
　　　every Saturday.
　　B. It doesn't look very safe
　　　to me.
　　C. I'm not in the mood to
　　　go fishing today.

三、言談理解（推論）

　　本部份共 10 題，每題光碟放音機會播出一段對話及一個相
關的問題，聽後從試題冊上 A、B、C 三個選項中，選出一個最
適合的回答。每題播出二遍。

例： （聽） (Man)　　May I help you?

（Woman)　Yes, I'd like to look at that red sweater.
How much is it?

(Man)　　It's one thousand dollars.

Question: Where are the man and the woman?

（看） A. In a restaurant.
B. In the living room.
C. In a department store.

正確答案爲 C，請在答案紙上塗黑作答。

21. A. Start a job.
B. Quit her job.
C. Have a job interview.

22. A. Save her seat.
B. Use the restroom.
C. Sit down.

23. A. For school.
B. For work.
C. To be closer to his family.

24. A. In a bank.
B. At the beach.
C. In a shoe store.

25. A. Luke.
B. Luke's mother.
C. Luke's father.

26. A. They are reading the same book.
B. They have reached an understanding.
C. They need more time to talk.

27. A. The man doesn't have a problem.
B. The woman is a bad cook.
C. He ate something bad for breakfast.

28. A. He doesn't wear a suit every day.
B. He is an excellent student.
C. He wants to be a teacher.

29. A. Stan didn't know what he was doing.
B. Stan isn't to blame for the failure.
C. The economy is prosperous.

30. A. The woman is rich.
B. He doesn't buy many things.
C. Banks are unreliable.

國中會考英文聽力 ⑧ 詳解

一、辨識句意

1. (**A**) Oscar is getting ready to throw the ball.
   奧斯卡準備好要投球。
   * throw〔θro〕*v.* 投；拋　　ball〔bɔl〕*n.* 球

2. (**B**) Tonight, let's study Chinese. 今晚，一起來學中文吧。
   * ***let's* + *V*.** 讓我們來～（= *let us* + *V*.）
   study〔'stʌdɪ〕*v.* 學習；研讀　　Chinese〔tʃaɪ'niz〕*n.* 中文

3. (**A**) May I borrow a pen? 我可以借支筆嗎？
   * borrow〔'bɔro〕*v.* 借（入）　　pen〔pɛn〕*n.* 筆

4. (**C**) There is a calendar on the wall. 牆上有日曆。
   * calendar〔'kæləndɚ〕*n.* 日曆；月曆

5. (**B**) There is a map on the wall. 牆上有地圖。
   * map〔mæp〕*n.* 地圖

6. (**B**) Let's have our lunch sitting by the fountain.
   讓我們坐在噴水池旁吃午餐吧。
   * lunch〔lʌntʃ〕*n.* 午餐　　fountain〔'faʊntn̩〕*n.* 噴水池；噴泉

7. (**B**) There is a painting on the wall. 牆上有一幅畫。
   * paiting〔'pentɪŋ〕*n.* 圖畫

8. (**C**) Our school has a curved roof. 我們學校的屋頂是弧形的。
   * curved〔kɜvd〕*adj.* 彎曲的；弧形的
   roof〔ruf〕*n.* 屋頂

9. (**A**) I live in the city.　我住在城市裡。

　　　* city〔'sɪtɪ〕n. 城市

10. (**C**) Mr. Poole is an excellent cook.　普勒先生是個優秀的廚師。

　　　* excellent〔'ɛksḷənt〕adj. 極棒的；優秀的
　　　cook〔kʊk〕n. 廚師

二、基本問答

11. (**A**) What's that you're listening to?　I've never heard that
　　　singer's voice before.

　　　你在聽什麼？我之前從未聽過那歌手的聲音。

　　　A. The latest song by Justin Bieber, "Move It."
　　　　賈斯汀畢柏的最新歌曲「動起來」。
　　　B. I like it, too.　我也喜歡。
　　　C. My sister gave it to me.　我妹妹給我的。

　　　* *listen to* 聽　　　voice〔vɔɪs〕n. 聲音
　　　latest〔'letɪst〕adj. 最新的
　　　Justin Bieber 賈斯汀畢柏【美國流行男偶像歌手】

12. (**B**) Wow!　You look great!　Have you lost weight?

　　　哇！你看起來很棒！你減重了嗎？

　　　A. That's your problem.　那是你的問題。
　　　B. Yes, I've lost twelve pounds.　Can you tell?
　　　　是的，我減了十二磅，你看得出來嗎？
　　　C. It used to be blonde.　以前是金髮。

　　　* look〔lʊk〕v. 看起來　　weight〔wet〕n. 體重
　　　lose weight 減重
　　　pound〔paʊnd〕n. 磅【重量單位，一磅為 0.45 公斤】
　　　tell〔tɛl〕v. 看得出來；判斷　　*used to* 以前
　　　blonde〔blɑnd〕adj. 金髮的

13. (**A**) Can you tell me how to get to the bus station?

你可以告訴我要如何去公車站嗎？

A. I wish I could. Sorry, I'm not from around here either.
<u>我希望我可以。抱歉，但我也不是住這附近。</u>

B. I wouldn't do that if I were you.
如果我是你，我不會那麼做。

C. Yes, he's right over there. 是的，他就在那裡。

* ***get to*** 到達   ***bus station*** 公車站

14. (**C**) Hi, Maggie. How's your new job going?

嗨，瑪姬，妳的新工作如何？

A. I'm not sure if it works. Let me check.
我不確定這有沒有用，讓我檢查看看。

B. It takes about an hour each way.
一趟要花大概一小時。

C. Not bad. I'm still getting used to it.
<u>不錯，我還在適應中。</u>

* go〔go〕*v.* 進展   ***How is ~ going?*** ～進展如何？
work〔wɜk〕*v.* 進行順利；有效
check〔tʃɛk〕*v.* 檢查；確認
take〔tek〕*v.* 花費（時間）   way〔we〕*n.* 路程；行程
not bad 不錯   ***get used to*** 習慣；適應

15. (**B**) Everybody is talking about the new version of Titanic in 3-D. Have you seen it?

每個人都在談論鐵達尼號的 3D 版，你看過了嗎？

A. That ship has sailed. 那艘船已經啟航了。

B. No. I'm not interested. <u>沒有，我沒興趣。</u>

C. You can't believe everything you see and hear.
你不能完全相信你所看到跟聽到的。

* version〔'vɝʒən〕n. 版本
  Titanic〔taɪ'tænɪk〕n. 鐵達尼號【英國豪華巨輪，於 1912 年的處女
  航撞上冰山而沈沒，此事後被翻拍成電影】
  3D 三維立體 (= *three dimensions*)
  sail〔sel〕v. 啓航；出港
  interested〔'ɪntrɪstɪd〕*adj.* 感興趣的

16. (**B**) Why are Olivia and Daniel going to Sunshine City?
     爲什麼奧莉維亞和丹尼爾要去太陽城？

　　A. It's always sunny in Sunshine City.
　　　　太陽城的天氣總是很晴朗。
　　B. To visit their grandparents. 去探訪他們的祖父母。
　　C. There's Olivia and Daniel. 奧莉維亞和丹尼爾在那裡。

　　* sunshine〔'sʌn,ʃaɪn〕n. 陽光　　sunny〔'sʌnɪ〕*adj.* 晴朗的
　　grandparents〔'grænd,pɛrənts〕*n. pl.* 祖父母

17. (**B**) Do you believe it is bad luck to walk under a ladder?
     你相信從梯子下面走過會帶來惡運嗎？

　　A. Sure, if you do it right. 當然，如果你做對了的話。
　　B. No, that's just a superstition. 不，那只是個迷信。
　　C. Who broke the mirror? 誰打破了鏡子？

　　* ***bad luck*** 惡運　　ladder〔'lædə〕n. 梯子
　　superstition〔,supə'stɪʃən〕n. 迷信　　break〔brek〕v. 打破
　　mirror〔'mɪrə〕n. 鏡子

18. (**A**) Is it hot in here or is it just me? 是這裡太熱，還是我的問題？

　　A. Yes, it's boiling. Turn down the heat.
　　　　是的，很熱，把暖氣關小。
　　B. Yes, I can see it too. Your turn.
　　　　是的，我也可以看到，該你了。
　　C. No, it's just you. Put on a sweater.
　　　　不，是你的問題，把毛衣穿上。

* boiling (ˈbɔɪlɪŋ) *adj.* 沸騰的；酷熱的
turn down 把（電器、火）關小
heat (hit) *n.* 暖氣　　turn (tɜn) *n.* 輪流
put on 穿上　　sweater (ˈswɛtɚ) *n.* 毛衣

19. (**A**) Hi, Nancy. Do you have plans this Sunday?

嗨，南西，這週日有計畫嗎？

　　A. No, I don't. 不，沒有。

　　B. No, I can't. 不，我不行。

　　C. No, I will. 不，我會。

　　* plan (plæn) *n.* 計畫

20. (**B**) Can we swim in this river? 我們可以在這條河裡游泳嗎？

　　A. I have swim lessons every Saturday.

　　　　我每週六都有游泳課。

　　B. It doesn't look very safe to me. 這在我看來不太安全。

　　C. I'm not in the mood to go fishing today.

　　　　我今天沒心情去釣魚。

　　* river (ˈrɪvɚ) *n.* 河流　　lesson (ˈlɛsn̩) *n.* 課程
　　look (lʊk) *v.* 看起來　　safe (sef) *adj.* 安全的
　　mood (mud) *n.* 心情　　**be in the mood to** + **V.** 有心情做～
　　go fishing 去釣魚

三、言談理解

21. (**C**) M : Hi, Suzie. When is your job interview?

　　男：嗨，蘇西，妳何時要面試工作？

　　W : It's tomorrow. I'm so nervous.

　　女：明天，我好緊張。

　　M : You'll do just fine.

　　男：妳會表現得很好的。

Question : What will Suzie do tomorrow?

　　　　　蘇西明天要做什麼？

A. Start a job. 開始工作。

B. Quit her job. 辭職。

C. Have a job interview. 面試工作。

* job〔dʒɑb〕*n.* 工作
  interview〔'ɪntɚ,vju〕*n.* 面談；面試
  nervous〔'nɝvəs〕*adj.* 緊張的
  do〔du〕*v.* 表現；進展
  fine〔faɪn〕*adv.* 很好地
  quit〔kwɪt〕*v.* 停止；放棄

22. (**C**) W : Excuse me, sir. Is this seat taken?

　　　　　女：先生，很抱歉，這座位有人坐嗎？

　　　　　M : I'm afraid it is, miss. My wife is in the restroom and
　　　　　　　will return shortly.

　　　　　男：恐怕有，小姐。我妻子在洗手間，不久就會回來。

　　　　　W : I see. Sorry to disturb you.

　　　　　女：我知道了，不好意思打擾你。

　　　　　Question : What does the woman want to do?

　　　　　　　　　　女士想做什麼？

A. Save her seat. 保留她的位子。

B. Use the restroom. 使用洗手間。

C. Sit down. 坐下來。

* seat〔sit〕*n.* 座位
  afraid〔ə'fred〕*adj.*（感覺遺憾）恐怕…
  restroom〔'rɛst,rum〕*n.* 洗手間；廁所
  return〔rɪ'tɝn〕*v.* 返回
  shortly〔'ʃɔrtlɪ〕*adv.* 不久；很快
  disturb〔dɪ'stɝb〕*v.* 打擾　　save〔sev〕*v.* 保留

23. (**B**) M : I heard you're moving to Taichung.　Is that true?

男： 我聽說妳要搬到台中，是真的嗎？

W : Yes, I've got a great job offer.　Why do you seem surprised?

女： 是的，我應徵到一個很棒的工作。你怎麼看似很驚訝？

M : Oh, never mind.　Best of luck to you.

男： 喔，別在意，祝妳好運。

Question : Why is the woman moving to Taichung?

為何女士即將搬到台中？

A. For school.　為了上學。

B. For work.　為了工作。

C. To be closer to his family.　為了要和家人住比較近。

* move〔muv〕v. 搬家　　offer〔'ɔfɚ〕n. 提議；提供
  job offer 錄用信　　seem〔sim〕v. 看似
  surprised〔sə'praɪzd〕adj. 驚訝的
  mind〔maɪnd〕v. 在意；介意
  never mind 沒關係；別介意
  best of luck to sb. 祝某人好運

24. (**C**) W : May I help you?

女： 需要我幫忙嗎？

M : Yes.　Do you have these shoes in a size eleven?

男： 是的，這雙鞋子有十一號嗎？

W : Everything we have in stock is on the rack.

女： 我們所有的存貨都在架上。

Question : Where are the speakers?　說話者在哪裡？

A. In a bank.　在銀行裡。

B. At the beach.　在沙灘上。

C. In a shoe store.　在鞋店裡。

* size〔saɪz〕*n.* 尺寸　　stock〔stɑk〕*n.* 存貨
in stock 有存貨；有現貨
rack〔ræk〕*n.*（擺設東西用的）架子
bank〔bæŋk〕*n.* 銀行　　beach〔bitʃ〕*n.* 沙灘

25. (**B**) M：Hi, Ms. Thorp. This is Michael. May I speak with Luke?

男：嗨，索普女士，我是麥可，我可以和路克講話嗎？

W：He's not home right now, honey. Would you like to leave a message?

女：親愛的，他現在不在家，你要留言嗎？

M：Would you please tell him I called?

男：可以請妳告訴他我打過電話來嗎？

Question：Who is Michael most likely speaking with?

麥可最可能是和誰講話？

A. Luke. 路克。

B. Luke's mother. 路克的母親。

C. Luke's father. 路克的父親。

* ***This is ~.*** 我是～。（用於講電話）
message〔ˈmɛsɪdʒ〕*n.* 訊息；留言　　***leave a message*** 留言

26. (**B**) W：This was a very good idea, Frank. I'm glad we had the chance to talk.

女：法蘭克，這是個很好的主意。我很高興我們有機會聊聊。

M：Yes, me too, Ms. Moore.

男：是的，我也這麼覺得，莫爾女士。

W：I think we're on the same page now. Is there anything else to discuss?

女：我覺得我們有共識了，有什麼其他的要討論嗎？

Question：What does the woman imply? 女士暗示什麼？

A. They are reading the same book. 他們正在讀同一本書。

B. They have reached an understanding. 他們達成協議了。

C. They need more time to talk. 他們需要更多時間聊聊。

* glad〔glæd〕adj. 高興的　　chance〔tʃæns〕n. 機會
page〔pedʒ〕n.（書的）頁
be on the same page 達到共識（= *understand each other*）
discuss〔dɪ'skʌs〕v. 討論　　imply〔ɪm'plaɪ〕v. 暗示
reach〔ritʃ〕v. 達成（結論、協議）
understanding〔͵ʌndɚ'stændɪŋ〕n. 約定；了解
reach an understanding 達成協議

27. (**A**) M：What's going on? You look awful!

男：發生什麼事了？妳看起來不太舒服！

W：It's my stomach. I think I ate something bad for breakfast.

女：我的胃不舒服，我覺得我早餐吃錯東西了

M：Really? But we ate at the same place and I feel fine.

男：真的嗎？但我們在同一個地方吃東西，我覺得沒問題。

Question：What is the man's problem? 男士的問題是什麼？

A. The man doesn't have a problem. 男士不覺得有問題。

B. The woman is a bad cook. 女士廚藝很差。

C. He ate something bad for breakfast.

　　他早餐吃了不好的東西。

* *go on* 發生　　awful〔'ɔful〕adj. 可怕的；不舒服的
stomach〔'stʌmək〕n. 胃　　breakfast〔'brɛkfəst〕n. 早餐
cook〔kʊk〕n. 廚師

28. (**A**) W：Tom looks very handsome in that suit.

女：湯姆穿那套西裝很帥。

M : Why is he dressed up today? Does he have some important event?

男：他爲何今天盛裝打扮？他有什麼重要的事情嗎？

W : He's giving a presentation in his computer class.

女：他即將要在電腦課上做簡報。

Question : What can be assumed about Tom?

關於湯姆我們可以做何推論？

A. He doesn't wear a suit every day.

<u>他不會天天穿西裝。</u>

B. He is an excellent student. 他是個優秀的學生。

C. He wants to be a teacher. 他想要當老師。

* handsome〔'hænsəm〕*adj.* 英俊的　suit〔sut〕*n.* 西裝
be dressed up 盛裝打扮　event〔ɪ'vɛnt〕*n.* 大事；事件
presentation〔ˌprɛzn̩'teʃən〕*n.* 報告；發表（演講）
give a presentation 做簡報
assume〔ə'sjum〕*v.* 假定；認爲
excellent〔'ɛksl̩ənt〕*adj.* 優秀的

29. (**B**) M : Did you hear that Stan's café went out of business?

男：妳知道史丹的咖啡館停止營業了嗎？

W : No, I didn't. What happened? Stan seemed like he knew what he was doing.

女：不，我不知道。怎麼了？史丹看似清楚自己在做什麼。

M : I don't think it was Stan's fault. This economy is killing small businesses.

男：我不覺得這是史丹的錯，現在的經濟狀況毀了許多小型的行業。

Question : What does the man say? 男士說了什麼？

A. Stan didn't know what he was doing.
史丹不知道自己在做什麼。

B. Stan isn't to blame for the failure.
失敗不是史丹造成的。

C. The economy is prosperous. 經濟很繁榮。

* business〔'bɪznɪs〕 n. 行業；營業　café〔kə'fe〕 n. 咖啡店
  out of business 停業；倒閉　fault〔fɔlt〕 n. 過錯
  economy〔ɪ'kɑnəmɪ〕 n. 經濟　kill〔kɪl〕 v. 消滅；破壞
  blame〔blem〕 v. 責備；歸咎
  be to blame for 為…負責　failure〔'feljɚ〕 n. 失敗
  prosperous〔'prɑspərəs〕 adj. 繁榮的

30. (**A**) M：Can I borrow some money?
男：我可以借一些錢嗎？

W：I'm sorry. I've only got one hundred dollars in my
bank account.
女：很抱歉，我銀行戶頭只有一百元。

M：You? Ms. Moneybags only has a hundred bucks? I
don't buy it.【詳見背景說明】
男：妳？財富小姐居然只有一百元？我不相信。

Question：What does the man imply? 男士暗示什麼？

A. The woman is rich. 女士很有錢。

B. He doesn't buy many things. 他不會買很多東西。

C. Banks are unreliable. 銀行不可靠。

* borrow〔'bɑro〕 v. 借（入）
  bank〔bæŋk〕 n. 銀行　account〔ə'kaʊnt〕 n. 帳戶
  moneybags〔'mʌnɪ,bægz〕 n. （可當單數或複數用）財富；
    有錢人；大財主
  buck〔bʌk〕 n. 一美元　buy〔baɪ〕 v. 買；相信
  rich〔rɪtʃ〕 adj. 有錢的　unreliable〔,ʌnrɪ'laɪəbl〕 adj. 不可靠的

國中會考英文聽力⑨

一、辨識句意

本部分共 10 題，每題有三個圖片選項，請聽光碟放音機播出的題目，聽後從試題冊上 A、B、C 圖片中，選出一個最適合的回答。每題播出二遍。

例：（聽）John enjoys taking a bath.
　　（看）

<table>
<tr><td>(A)</td><td>(B)</td><td>(C)</td></tr>
</table>

正確答案爲 C，請在答案紙上塗黑作答。

1.　A.　　　　　B.　　　　　C.

2.　A.　　　　　B.　　　　　C.

 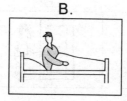 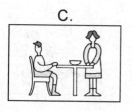

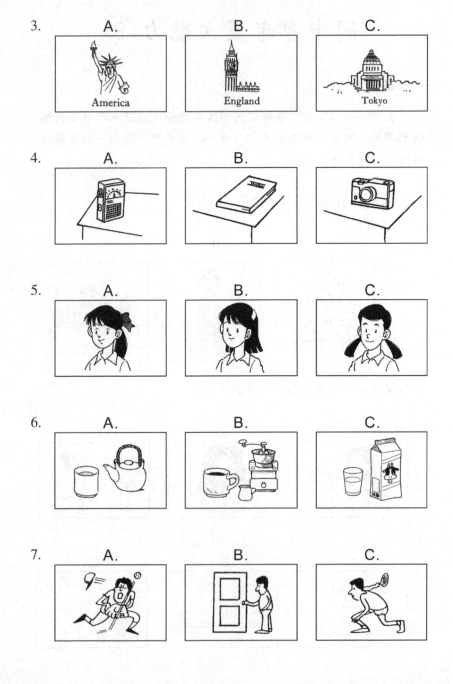

3.
A.
America

B.
England

C.
Tokyo

4.
A.

B.

C.

5.
A.

B.

C.

6.
A.

B.

C.

7.
A.

B.

C.

8.　A.　　　　　B.　　　　　C.

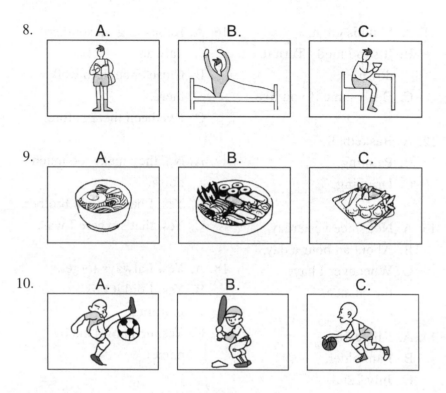

9.　A.　　　　　B.　　　　　C.

10.　A.　　　　　B.　　　　　C.

二、**基本問答**：選出最適合的回答，完成對話。

　　本部份共 10 題，每題光碟放音機會播出一個問句或直述句，聽後從試題冊上 A、B、C 三個選項中，選出一個最適合的回答。每題播出二遍。

　例：（聽）Hi, Mike. I haven't seen you for a long time.
　　　　　　 How are you doing?

　　　（看）A. I'm watching TV.
　　　　　　 B. I'm OK, thanks.
　　　　　　 C. I'm at school.

　　正確答案為 B，請在答案紙上塗黑作答。

11. A. Sounds great.
    B. It's too loud. Turn it down.
    C. Have some if you like.

12. A. Basketball.
    B. Painting.
    C. Drinking.

13. A. Not since yesterday.
    B. About an hour a day.
    C. Whenever I have the chance.

14. A. I'll be 16.
    B. I am older.
    C. July 22nd.

15. A. No, my parents don't give me an allowance.
    B. Maybe I can let you have it if you want.
    C. Yes, I work at the campus bookstore.

16. A. Kaohsiung, in southern Taiwan.
    B. Close enough to walk there.
    C. I've been there before.

17. A. No, they make too much noise.
    B. Yes, I have a twin brother.
    C. Yes, that's where I was.

18. A. Yes, I always forget.
    B. Yes, I did it this morning.
    C. Yes, he knows me by name.

19. A. Yes, I got one for you.
    B. No, it's here forever.
    C. Most are, yes.

20. A. We're almost there.
    B. It closes at dusk.
    C. No, don't go there.

三、言談理解（推論）

　　本部份共 10 題，每題光碟放音機會播出一段對話及一個相關的問題，聽後從試題冊上 A、B、C 三個選項中，選出一個最適合的回答。每題播出二遍。

例： （聽）　(Man)　　May I help you?

　　　　　(Woman)　Yes, I'd like to look at that red sweater.
　　　　　　　　　How much is it?

　　　　　(Man)　　It's one thousand dollars.

　　　　Question: Where are the man and the woman?

（看）　A. In a restaurant.

　　　　B. In the living room.

　　　　C. In a department store.

正確答案為 C，請在答案紙上塗黑作答。

21. A. She read a book.
　　B. She went to a party.
　　C. She watched a movie.

22. A. The restroom is hard to find.
　　B. The restroom is filthy.
　　C. The restroom is occupied.

23. A. The man.
　　B. The woman.
　　C. The landlord.

24. A. She is a fussy eater.
　　B. She has a new boyfriend.
　　C. She is beautiful.

25. A. They will go to the night market.
　　B. The man will try on the sunglasses.
　　C. The woman will make a deal.

26. A. Hold the ladder.
　　B. Climb the ladder.
　　C. Change the light bulb.

27. A. She did see the pandas.
　　B. Her family didn't want to.
　　C. The wait was too long.

28. A. Give the man a signal.
　　B. Make a phone call.
　　C. Read the dial on her clock.

29. A. The man.
　　B. The woman.
　　C. It is impossible to say.

30. A. Be quiet.
　　B. Take a nap.
　　C. Go outside and play.

國中會考英文聽力 ⑨ 詳解

一、辨識句意

1. (**A**) Olivia is enjoying a meal. 奧莉維亞正在享用餐點。
   * enjoy〔ɪn'dʒɔɪ〕v. 享受
   meal〔mil〕n. 餐點；一餐

2. (**B**) Mr. Liu is ready for bed. 劉先生準備要上床睡覺。
   * **be ready for** 準備好~　　　bed〔bɛd〕n. 就寢（時間）

3. (**C**) I'll spend the summer in Tokyo. 我會在東京度過夏季。
   * spend〔spɛnd〕v. 度過（時間、假期）
   summer〔'sʌmɚ〕n. 夏天；夏季
   Tokyo〔'tokɪo〕n. 東京【日本首都】

4. (**C**) My camera is on the table. 我的相機在桌上。
   * camera〔'kæmərə〕n. 照相機；攝影機　　table〔'tebl̩〕n. 桌子

5. (**A**) Victoria is wearing a pretty bow in her hair.
   維多利亞頭髮戴著美麗的蝴蝶結。
   * wear〔wɛr〕v. 穿著；戴著　　bow〔bo〕n. 蝴蝶結

6. (**A**) Would you like a cup of tea? 你想要喝杯茶嗎？
   * cup〔kʌp〕n. 杯子；一杯的量　　tea〔ti〕n. 茶

7. (**B**) Brad is closing the door. 布萊德正在關門。
   * close〔kloz〕v. 關（門、窗戶）

8. (**A**) Mr. Lee is reading a book. 李先生在讀書。
   * read〔rid〕v. 閱讀

9. (**B**) Let's have sushi for dinner tonight. 今晚我們來吃壽司吧。

     * **let's + V.** 讓我們來～ (= *let us*)

       have〔hæv〕*v.* 吃；喝   sushi〔'susɪ〕*n.* 壽司

10. (**A**) Richard enjoys playing soccer. 理查喜歡踢足球。

     * **enjoy + V-ing** 喜愛～   soccer〔'sɑkɚ〕*n.* 足球

二、基本問答

11. (**A**) I'm starving. How does Italian food sound tonight?

     我餓死了，今晚吃義大利菜如何？

     A. Sounds great. 聽起來很棒。

     B. It's too loud. Turn it down. 太大聲了，關小聲點。

     C. Have some if you like. 如果你喜歡的話，就吃一點。

     * starve〔stɑrv〕*v.* 感到飢餓

       Italian〔ɪ'tæljən〕*adj.* 義大利的

       sound〔saʊnd〕*v.* 聽起來

       loud〔laʊd〕*adj.* 大聲的

       turn down （收音機等）關小聲

12. (**A**) I really love playing volleyball. What is your favorite sport?

     我真的很喜歡打排球，你最喜愛的運動是什麼？

     A. Basketball. 籃球。

     B. Painting. 畫畫。

     C. Drinking. 喝酒。

     * volleyball〔'vɑlɪ,bɔl〕*n.* 排球（運動）

       favorite〔'fevərɪt〕*adj.* 最喜歡的   sport〔sport〕*n.* 運動

       basketball〔'bæskɪt,bɔl〕*n.* 籃球

       paint〔pent〕*v.* 繪畫

13. (**C**) How often do you surf the Internet?　你多久上網一次？

　　A. Not since yesterday.　從昨天開始就沒有了。

　　B. About an hour a day.　一天大約一小時。

　　C. Whenever I have the chance.　每當我有機會的時候。

　　* **how often** 多久一次　　surf〔sɝf〕v. 瀏覽（網路）；上（網）
　　Internet〔ˋɪntɚˏnɛt〕n. 網際網路
　　whenever〔hwɛnˋɛvɚ〕conj. 每當…的時候

14. (**C**) I can't believe I'm turning 16 tomorrow.　When is your birthday, Gem?

　　我無法相信我明天就要十六歲了，珍，妳生日何時？

　　A. I'll be 16.　我將要十六歲。

　　B. I am older.　我比較年長。

　　C. July 22nd.　七月二十二日。

　　* believe〔bəˋliv〕v. 相信　　turn〔tɝn〕v. 變成

15. (**C**) You always have money, Henry.　You must have a part-time job.

　　亨利，你總是有錢，你一定有兼職工作。

　　A. No, my parents don't give me an allowance.
　　　不，我父母不給我零用錢。

　　B. Maybe I can let you have it if you want.
　　　如果你要或許我可以給你。

　　C. Yes, I work at the campus bookstore.
　　　是的，我在學校的書店工作。

　　* part-time〔ˋpartˏtaɪm〕adj. 兼職的；兼任的
　　job〔dʒab〕n. 工作
　　allowance〔əˋlaʊəns〕n. 零用錢
　　campus〔ˋkæmpəs〕n. 校園
　　bookstore〔ˋbʊkˏstor〕n. 書店；書局

16. (**A**) It's nice to meet you, Nelson. Where are you from?
很高興認識你，尼爾森。你來自哪裡？

    A. Kaohsiung, in southern Taiwan. <u>南台灣的高雄。</u>

    B. Close enough to walk there.
       近到用走的就到了。

    C. I've been there before. 我之前去過那裡。

    * meet〔mit〕*v.* 認識   southern〔'sʌðən〕*adj.* 南方的
      enough to + V. …而足以～

17. (**A**) My sister just had twins. Do you enjoy being around
children? 我姊姊剛生了雙胞胎，你喜歡跟小孩在一起嗎？

    A. No, they make too much noise.
      <u>不，他們會很吵。</u>

    B. Yes, I have a twin brother.
      是的，我有個雙胞胎弟弟。

    C. Yes, that's where I was.
      是的，我在那裡。

    * twin〔twɪn〕*n.* 雙胞胎之一   *adj.* 雙胞胎的
      noise〔nɔɪz〕*n.* 噪音

18. (**B**) Did you remember to make an appointment to see the
dentist? 你有記得要預約去看牙醫嗎？

    A. Yes, I always forget. 有，我總是忘記。

    B. Yes, I did it this morning. <u>有，我今天早上約了。</u>

    C. Yes, he knows me by name. 有，他知道我的名字。

    * appoinment〔ə'pɔɪntmənt〕*n.* 約定；預約
      make an appointment 預約
      dentist〔'dɛntɪst〕*n.* 牙醫
      know sb. ***by name*** （未見過面）只知道名字

19. (**C**) Many kids seem to be getting tattoos lately. Are tattoos permanent?

很多小孩最近似乎都在刺青，刺青是永久的嗎？

A. Yes, I got one for you. 是的，我幫你拿一個。

B. No, it's here forever. 不，它永遠會在這。

C. Most are, yes. 大多數是的。

* kid〔kɪd〕*n.* 小孩   seem〔sim〕*v.* 似乎
tattoo〔tæ'tu〕*n.* 刺青
permanent〔'pɜmənənt〕*adj.* 永久的
forever〔fə'ɛvə〕*adv.* 永久地

20. (**A**) We've been driving for an hour. How much farther is it to the lake?

我們已經開一小時的車了，還要多遠才會到湖邊？

A. We're almost there. 我們快到了。

B. It closes at dusk. 黃昏時關門。

C. No, don't go there. 不，別去那裡。

* drive〔draɪv〕*v.* 開車   further〔'fɑrðə〕*adv.* 更遠
lake〔lek〕*n.* 湖   dusk〔dʌsk〕*n.* 黃昏   *at dusk* 黃昏時

三、言談理解

21. (**C**) M：What did you do last night?

男：妳昨天做了什麼？

W：Not much. I stayed home and watched a movie.

女：沒做什麼，我待在家看電影。

M：I thought you were going to the party with Jill.

男：我以為妳和吉兒去派對。

Question：What did the woman do last night?

女士昨晚做了什麼？

A.　She read a book.　她讀書。

B.　She went to a party.　她去派對。

C.　She watched a movie.　<u>她看電影。</u>

＊ ***watch a movie*** 看電影　　 party〔ˋpɑrtɪ〕*n.* 派對

22.（ **A** ）W：Do you know where the restroom is?

女：你知道洗手間在哪裡嗎？

M：Go up these stairs, down the hall, and it's the third door on the right.

男：走這些樓梯上去，沿著走廊走，在右邊第三個門。

W：Good Lord, can you draw me a map?

女：天啊，你可以畫張地圖給我嗎？

Question：What does the woman imply?

女士暗示什麼？

A.　The restroom is hard to find.　<u>洗手間很難找。</u>

B.　The restroom is filthy.　洗手間很髒。

C.　The restroom is occupied.　洗手間有人在用。

＊ restroom〔ˋrɛstˏrum〕*n.* 洗手間；廁所
　 stair〔stɛr〕*n.* 樓梯　　 ***go up the stairs*** 上樓梯
　 hall〔hɔl〕*n.* 走廊　　 ***Good Lord!*** 天啊！
　 map〔mæp〕*n.* 地圖　　 filthy〔ˋfɪlθɪ〕*adj.* 髒的
　 occupied〔ˋɑkjəˏpaɪd〕*adj.* 被佔據的；使用中的

23.（ **C** ）M：Why is it so hot in here?

男：為什麼這裡這麼熱？

W：The air-conditioner broke down again.

女：冷氣機又故障了。

M：Did you call the landlord? This is unbearable.

男：妳有打電話給房東嗎？這令人難以忍受。

Question : Who is most likely responsible for fixing the
air-conditioner? 誰最有可能負責修理冷氣？

A. The man. 男士。

B. The woman. 女士。

C. The landlord. 房東。

* air-conditioner *n.* 冷氣；空調　　***break down*** 故障
landlord〔ˈlændˏlɔrd〕*n.* 房東
unberable〔ʌnˈbɛrəb!〕*adj.* 難以忍受的
responsible〔rɪˈspɑnsəb!〕*adj.* 負責的
be responsible for 對⋯負責　　fix〔fɪks〕*v.* 修理

24. (**B**) W : Is Amy coming to dinner?

女： 愛咪要來吃晚餐嗎？

M : Yes, and she's bringing her new boyfriend.

男： 是的，她會帶她的新男朋友過來。

W : Really? I can't wait to meet him.

女： 真的嗎？我等不及要看到他。

Question : What do we know about Amy?

我們可以知道愛咪的什麼事？

A. She is a fussy eater. 她是個挑剔的食客。

B. She has a new boyfriend. 她有新男友。

C. She is beautiful. 她很美。

* ***can't wait to + V.*** 等不及要～　　fussy〔ˈfʌsɪ〕*adj.* 愛挑剔的

25. (**B**) M : Those are cool sunglasses. Where did you get them?

男： 這些太陽眼鏡好酷，你在哪裡買的？

W : At the night market. They were only NT$100.

女： 在夜市，只要台幣一百元。

M : Wow! Such a great deal. Can I try them on?

男：哇！好划算，我可以戴看看嗎？

Question : What will probably happen next?

接下來可能會發生什麼事？

A. They will go to the night market. 他們會去夜市。

B. The man will try on the sunglasses.

<u>男士會戴上太陽眼鏡。</u>

C. The woman will make a deal. 女士會完成一筆交易。

* sunglasses〔ˈsʌnˌglæsɪz〕*n. pl.* 太陽眼鏡

　night market 夜市　　cost〔kɔst〕*v.* (事物) 花費

　deal〔dil〕*n.* 交易　　*a great deal* 很划算

　try on 試穿；試戴　　next〔nɛkst〕*adv.* 接下來

　make a deal 完成一筆交易

26. (**C**) W : What is Jack trying to do?

女：傑克想要做什麼？

M : It looks like he's trying to change a light bulb.

男：他好像要換燈泡。

W : He'd better be careful. That ladder looks very shaky.

女：他最好小心點，梯子看起來搖搖晃晃的。

Question : What is Jack trying to do? 傑克想要做什麼？

A. Hold the ladder. 握住梯子。

B. Climb the ladder. 爬梯子。

C. Change the light bulb. <u>換燈泡。</u>

* *it looks like* ～ 似乎～　　bulb〔bʌlb〕*n.* 燈泡

　light bulb 燈泡　　*had better* + *V.* 最好～

　careful〔ˈkɛrfəl〕*adj.* 小心的　　ladder〔ˈlædɚ〕*n.* 梯子

　shaky〔ˈʃekɪ〕*adj.* 搖晃的

　climb〔klaɪm〕*v.* 爬；登上

27. (**A**) M：Did you go to the zoo this weekend?

男：妳這週末有去動物園嗎？

W：Yes. I went with my family. We saw the pandas. They're so cute!

女：有，我跟我家人一起去。我們看到了貓熊，牠們好可愛！

M：Last time I was there, the wait to see them was over an hour.

男：我上次去動物園，要看牠們得等超過一小時。

Question：Why didn't the woman see the pandas?

女士為何沒看到貓熊？

A. She did see the pandas. 她真的有看到貓熊。

B. Her family didn't want to. 她的家人不想看。

C. The wait was too long. 等待時間很長。

* zoo〔zu〕*n.* 動物園　　weekend〔'wik'ɛnd〕*n.* 週末
　panda〔'pændə〕*n.* 貓熊　　cute〔kjut〕*adj.* 可愛的
　wait〔wet〕*n.* 等待；等待的時間
　do + V. 真的～；的確～

28. (**B**) W：Ah! I'm so frustrated.

女：啊！我覺得好沮喪。

M：What's wrong?

男：怎麼了？

W：I can't get a good cell phone signal, so I can't dial out.

女：我的手機訊號不好，所以我撥不出去。

Question：What is the woman trying to do?

女士試著要做什麼？

A. Give the man a signal. 給男子信號。

B. Make a phone call. 打電話。

C. Read the dial on her clock.

　　看她時鐘的鐘面。

* ah〔ɑ〕*interj.* 啊；哦　　frustrated〔'frʌstretɪd〕*adj.* 受挫的
  What's wrong? 怎麼了？　　***cell phone*** 手機
  signal〔'sɪgnl̩〕*n.* 信號；暗號　　read〔rid〕*v.* 查看；判讀
  dial〔'daɪəl〕*v.* 撥（電話）　*n.* 鐘面；錶面
  make a phone call 打電話　　clock〔klɑk〕*n.* 時鐘

29. (**A**) M：How many times have you been to Taipei 101?

　　　男：妳去過台北 101 幾次？

　　　W：Actually, this will be my first time.

　　　女：事實上，這將是我的第一次。

　　　M：Oh, I thought you'd been before. You're in for a treat.
　　　　　The view is incredible.

　　　男：喔，我以為妳之前去過。妳會喜歡的，這裡的景觀很棒。

　　　Question：Who has been to Taipei 101 before?

　　　　　　　誰去過台北 101？

　　　A. The man. 男士。

　　　B. The woman. 女士。

　　　C. It is impossible to say. 很難說。

* time〔taɪm〕*n.* 次數　　***have been to*** 曾經去過
  actually〔'æktʃuəlɪ〕*adv.* 實際上；事實上
  be in for 即將經歷
  treat〔trit〕*n.* 快樂；美好的事物
  You're in for a treat. 你（妳）會喜歡的。(= *You will enjoy it.*)
  view〔vju〕*n.* 視野；風景
  incredible〔ɪn'krɛdəbl̩〕*adj.* 令人無法置信的；了不起的；驚人的

30. (**A**) W : Would you mind keeping your voices down, boys?
　　　　　　　　I'm trying to take a nap.

女：男孩們，請你們把音量降低好嗎？我想要睡個午覺。

M : Sorry, Mom. We didn't realize you were trying
　　　to sleep.

男：媽，抱歉。我們不知道妳要睡覺。

W : That's OK. Just keep it down.

女：沒關係，就小聲點。

Question : What does the woman want the boys to do?
　　　　　母親要男孩們做什麼？

A. Be quiet. 安靜下來。

B. Take a nap. 睡午覺。

C. Go outside and play. 去外面玩。

＊mind〔maɪnd〕v. 介意
　Would you mind + V-ing? 請你（們）…好嗎？
　nap〔næp〕n. 小睡；午睡　　***take a nap*** 午睡；打盹
　realize〔'rɪəˌlaɪz〕v. 認知；瞭解
　keep down 壓低（聲音）　　quiet〔'kwaɪət〕adj. 安靜的

國中會考英文聽力 ⑩

一、辨識句意

　　本部分共 10 題，每題有三個圖片選項，請聽光碟放音機播出的題目，聽後從試題冊上 A、B、C 圖片中，選出一個最適合的回答。每題播出二遍。

例：　（聽）　John enjoys taking a bath.

　　　（看）

(A)　　　　　　　　(B)　　　　　　　　(C)

正確答案為 C，請在答案紙上塗黑作答。

1.　　A.　　　　　　　　B.　　　　　　　　C.

2.　　A.　　　　　　　　B.　　　　　　　　C.

3.　A.　　　　B.　　　　C.

4.　A.　　　　B.　　　　C.

5.　A.　　　　B.　　　　C.

6.　A.　　　　B.　　　　C.

7.　A.　　　　B.　　　　C.

8.
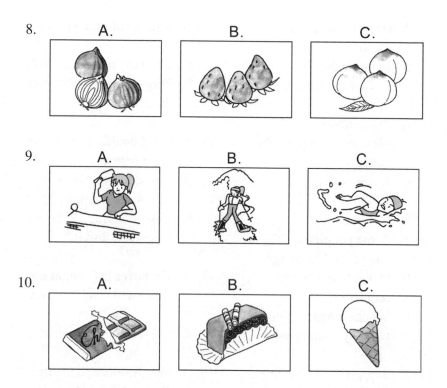

9.

10.

二、基本問答：選出最適合的回答，完成對話。

　　本部份共 10 題，每題光碟放音機會播出一個問句或直述句，聽後從試題冊上 A、B、C 三個選項中，選出一個最適合的回答。每題播出二遍。

例：（聽）Hi, Mike. I haven't seen you for a long time. How are you doing?

（看） A. I'm watching TV.
B. I'm OK, thanks.
C. I'm at school.

正確答案為 B，請在答案紙上塗黑作答。

11. A. He is a wonderful
person.
B. Jennifer did.
C. I saw John take it.

12. A. Three hours.
B. We don't accept credit
cards.
C. A one-way ticket is
$2000.

13. A. Some people say it is the
continental language.
B. Our school system
requires it.
C. When things are fun you
will enjoy them more.

14. A. Sure, it's half past nine.
B. I called to remind you.
C. There's one on my desk.

15. A. No thanks. I've got
everything under control.
B. There is no reason I can
think of.
C. They didn't say.

16. A. That's not how you spell
it.
B. I had the time of my life.
C. People are always saying
that.

17. A. No, I couldn't get a word
in edgewise.
B. I used to be able to hear
it, but not anymore.
C. Yes. It seemed to go on
forever, didn't it?

18. A. I'll never get caught up.
B. They will catch up with
us.
C. I'll take it spicy, please.

19. A. Was he close to the fire?
B. Well, it's probably in his
best interest.
C. He didn't want to fight.

20. A. I wouldn't even dream
of it.
B. No man is an island.
C. Yes, they will.

三、言談理解（推論）

　　本部份共 10 題，每題光碟放音機會播出一段對話及一個相
關的問題，聽後從試題冊上 A、B、C 三個選項中，選出一個最
適合的回答。每題播出二遍。

例： （聽）(Man)　　May I help you?

(Woman)　Yes, I'd like to look at that red sweater. How much is it?

(Man)　　It's one thousand dollars.

Question: Where are the man and the woman?

（看）A. In a restaurant.

B. In the living room.

C. In a department store.

正確答案爲 C，請在答案紙上塗黑作答。

21. A. I've heard this before.
    B. Whatever you want it to mean.
    C. Not very likely.

22. A. Julia's email address.
    B. Julia's phone number.
    C. Julia's address book.

23. A. Tornadoes.
    B. A small town.
    C. A television program about tornados.

24. A. The price is too high.
    B. The price is too low.
    C. The jeans are damaged.

25. A. What to eat tonight.
    B. What they ate yesterday.
    C. What they will eat tomorrow.

26. A. A restaurant.
    B. A movie theatre.
    C. A hotel.

27. A. Forecasting the weather.
    B. Reading a newspaper.
    C. Watching television.

28. A. Tokyo.
    B. Taiwan.
    C. It is impossible to say.

29. A. Brown.
    B. Blue.
    C. Green.

30. A. The man missed his flight.
    B. The man went to Los Angeles.
    C. The man checked in for his flight.

國中會考英文聽力 ⑩ 詳解

一、辨識句意

1. (**C**) Sunny has her hair in a ponytail. 桑尼把頭髮綁成馬尾。

    * ponytail〔'poni,tel〕*n.* 馬尾【髮結在腦後，讓頭髮自然下垂的髮型】

2. (**B**) Edward is washing his dog. 愛德華正在幫他的狗洗澡。

    * wash〔wɑʃ〕*v.* 洗

3. (**B**) William and Betty are going to class.

    威廉跟貝蒂一起去上課。

    * ***go to class*** 去上課

4. (**C**) Julie is playing tennis. 茱蒂在打網球。

    * tennis〔'tɛnɪs〕*n.* 網球

5. (**C**) Look! Harold caught a fish. 你看，海駱抓到一隻魚。

    * look〔luk〕*v.* 看；瞧【當感嘆詞用以引起對方的注意力】

    catch〔kætʃ〕*v.* 抓；捕捉【三態為：catch-caught-caught】

6. (**A**) Here, have some grapes. 在這，吃些葡萄吧。

    * have〔hæv〕*v.* 吃；喝   grape〔grep〕*n.* 葡萄

7. (**A**) Glen loves ice-skating. 葛藍喜歡溜冰。

    * ice-skate〔'aɪs,sket〕*v.* 溜冰

8. (**B**) Would you like some strawberries? 你想要些草莓嗎？

    * stawberry〔'strɔ,bɛrɪ〕*n.* 草莓

9. (**C**) Pamela is a good swimmer. 潘蜜拉很會游泳。

    * swimmer〔'swɪmɚ〕*n.* 游泳者

10. (**C**) Boy, I could really go for a scoop of ice cream.

　　　　當然，我真的可以再去拿一杓冰淇淋。

　　　　* boy〔bɔɪ〕*interj.* 真的的；當然【表示愉快、驚訝或諷刺的感嘆詞】
　　　　go for 拿；取　　scoop〔skup〕*n.* 一杓的量
　　　　ice cream 冰淇淋

二、基本問答

11. (**B**) Sorry, I'm late.　Do you know who won the contest?

　　　　抱歉，我遲到了。你知道誰贏了比賽嗎？

　　　　A.　He is a wonderful person.　他是個很棒的人。

　　　　B.　Jennifer did.　珍妮佛贏了。

　　　　C.　I saw John take it.　看到約翰拿走了。

　　　　* late〔let〕*adj.* 遲到的
　　　　win〔wɪn〕*v.* 贏【三態為：win-won-won】
　　　　contest〔'kɑntɛst〕*n.* 比賽
　　　　wonderful〔'wʌnfəfəl〕*adj.* 很棒的

12. (**C**) How much does it cost to fly to Japan?

　　　　坐飛機去日本要花多少錢？

　　　　A.　Three hours.　三小時。

　　　　B.　We don't accept credit cards.　我們不接受信用卡。

　　　　C.　A one-way ticket is $2000.　單程票是兩千元。

　　　　* fly〔flaɪ〕*v.* 搭飛機　　Japan〔dʒə'pæn〕*n.* 日本
　　　　credit card 信用卡　　***one-way*** *adj.* 單程的
　　　　one-way ticket 單程票

13. (**B**) There are many languages to choose from.　Why do you
　　　　study English?　有很多語言可以選擇，你為何讀英文？

　　　　A.　Some people say it is the continental language.

　　　　　　有些人說這是歐陸的語言。

B. Our school system requires it. <u>我們學校制度必修英文。</u>

C. When things are fun you will enjoy them more.

當事情是有趣的時候，你會更享受。

* language〔'læŋgwɪdʒ〕*n.* 語言　　***choose from*** 從…中選擇
continental〔ˌkɑntə'nɛntḷ〕*adj.* 歐洲大陸的
system〔'sɪstəm〕*n.* 體系；制度
require〔rɪ'kwaɪr〕*v.* 要求；規定　　fun〔fʌn〕*adj.* 有趣的

14. (**C**) May I borrow a pen? Mine just ran out of ink.

可以跟你借支筆嗎？我的沒墨水了。

A. Sure, it's half past nine. 當然，現在九點半。

B. I called to remind you. 我打電話是要提醒你。

C. There's one on my desk. <u>我書桌上有一支。</u>

* borrow〔'bɑro〕*v.* 借（入）　　pen〔pɛn〕*n.* 筆
ink〔ɪŋk〕*n.* 墨水　　***run out of*** 用完
remind〔rɪ'maɪnd〕*v.* 提醒；使想起　　desk〔dɛsk〕*n.* 書桌

15. (**A**) You look very busy, Alice. Is there anything I can do to
help? 愛麗絲，妳看起來很忙。我能幫什麼忙嗎？

A. No thanks. I've got everything under control.

<u>不，謝謝。一切都在掌握之中。</u>

B. There is no reason I can think of. 我想不到任何理由。

C. They didn't say. 他們沒說。

* look〔lʊk〕*v.* 看起來　　busy〔'bɪzɪ〕*adj.* 忙碌的
control〔kən'trol〕*n.* 控制
under control 控制之下　　reason〔'rizṇ〕*n.* 理由
think of 想到；想出

16. (**B**) Hi Jerome, glad to see you're back. How was your trip to
Hong Kong?

嗨，傑羅姆，很高興看到你回來。你的香港之旅如何？

A. That's not how you spell it. 那個字不是那樣拼的。

B. I had the time of my life. 我玩得非常愉快。【詳見背景説明】

C. People are always saying that. 人們總是這麼說。

* glad〔glæd〕*adj.* 高興的　　trip〔trɪp〕*n.* 旅行
  Hong Kong 香港　　spell〔spɛl〕*v.* 拼（字）
  have the time of *one's* ***life*** 過得愉快（= *have a good time*）

17. (**C**) Did you listen to the president's speech last night?
     你昨晚有聽總統的演講嗎？

    A. No, I couldn't get a word in edgewise. 不，我插不上嘴。

    B. I used to be able to hear it, but not anymore.
       我以前能夠聽到，現在不行了。

    C. Yes. It seemed to go on forever, didn't it?
       是的，看似沒完沒了，不是嗎？

    * ***listen to*** 聽　　president〔'prɛzədənt〕*n.* 總統
      speech〔spitʃ〕*n.* 演講
      edgewise〔'ɛdʒ,waɪz〕*adv.* 沿著邊
      get a word in edgewise 插嘴　　***used to*** 以前
      be able to + *V.* 能夠～　　***not anymore*** 不再
      go on 繼續下去　　forever〔fə'ɛvə〕*adv.* 永久地
      go on forever 持續下去；沒完沒了

18. (**C**) Would you prefer hot sauce or ketchup?
     你比較喜歡辣醬還是蕃茄醬？

    A. I'll never get caught up. 我永遠不會被追上。

    B. They will catch up with us. 他們會趕上我們。

    C. I'll take it spicy, please. 請給我辣的。

    * prefer〔prɪ'fɝ〕*v.* 比較喜歡　　sauce〔sɔs〕*n.* 醬；調味汁
      hot sauce 辣醬　　ketchup〔'kɛtʃəp〕*n.* 蕃茄醬
      catch up 追上　　***catch up with*** 趕上
      take〔tek〕*v.* 接受；接納　　spicy〔'spaɪsɪ〕*adj.* 辛辣的

19. (**B**) Derrick wanted to join the Army, but he failed the physical exam. 德瑞克想要從軍，但是沒過體檢。

A. Was he close to the fire? 他很靠近火場嗎？

B. Well, it's probably in his best interest.
嗯，這或許對他是好的。

C. He didn't want to fight. 他不想作戰。

* join〔dʒɔɪn〕v. 加入　　army〔ˋɑrmɪ〕n. 軍隊；陸軍
fail〔fel〕v. 不及格；未通過　　physical〔ˋfɪzɪkḷ〕adj. 身體的
exam〔ɪgˋzæm〕n. 考試；檢查（= examination）
fire〔faɪr〕n. 火；火災　　probably〔ˋprɑbəblɪ〕adv. 或許
interest〔ˋɪntrɪst〕n. 好處；利益
in one's (**best**) **interest** 爲了某人好；有利於某人
fight〔faɪt〕v. 作戰

20. (**A**) Would you ever cheat on an exam? 你考試會作弊嗎？

A. I wouldn't even dream of it. 我作夢也沒想過。

B. No man is an island. 沒有人是座孤島。

C. Yes, they will. 是的，他們會。

* cheat〔tʃit〕v. 欺騙；作弊　　**cheat on an exam** 考試作弊
dream〔drim〕v. 作夢；夢見　　**dream of** 夢到
island〔ˋaɪlənd〕n. 島
No man is an island.【諺】沒有人是座孤島。【表示人與社會休
戚與共，無法分離】

三、言談理解

21. (**C**) W：Are you going to Alex's party tonight?
女：你今晚要去愛力克斯的派對嗎？

M：Fat chance. We aren't on speaking terms.
男：希望很小，我們彼此不講話。

W：That's too bad. It sounds like it will be a fun party.
女：眞可惜，那聽起來好像會是個有趣的派對。

Question : What does "fat chance" mean?

　　　　　 "fat chance"是什麼意思？

A. I've heard this before. 我之前聽過。

B. Whatever you want it to mean.

　　任何你想要的意思。

C. Not very likely. 不太可能。

* party〔ˈpɑrtɪ〕*n.* 派對
  fat chance 希望很小；沒什麼希望
  too bad 真糟糕；真可惜
  terms〔tɜmz〕*n. pl.* 關係；情誼
  not on speaking terms 關係不好；不講話
  likely〔ˈlaɪklɪ〕*adj.* 可能的

22. (**B**) M : Do you know Julia's phone number?

男： 妳知道茱莉亞的電話嗎？

W : Not off the top of my head.　I left my address book at home.

女： 我一時想不到，我把通訊錄留在家裡了。

M : I've got to speak with her as soon as possible.

男： 我要能夠盡快跟她說些事情。

Question : What does the man want? 男子要什麼？

A. Julia's email address. 茱莉亞的電子郵件地址。

B. Julia's phone number. 茱莉亞的電話。

C. Julia's address book. 茱莉亞的通訊錄。

* *off the top of one's head* 不假思索地；馬上
  address〔ˈædrɛs〕*n.* 地址
  address book 通訊錄
  have got to + V. 必須～
  as ～ as possible 盡可能～
  email〔ˈiˌmel〕*n.* 電子郵件

23. (**A**) W : Did you watch the documentary on tornados last night?

女：你昨晚有看關於龍捲風的紀錄片嗎？

M : Yes, it was scary to see how entire towns get wiped out. Tornadoes can be very powerful.

男：有呀，看到整個城鎮都被摧毀眞是太可怕了。龍捲風威力可以很強大。

W : And they happen without warning. People barely have time to find shelter.

女：而且它們沒有預警就到來，人們幾乎沒有時間找到庇護所。

Question : What are the speakers mainly discussing?

說話者主要在討論什麼？

A. Tornadoes. 龍捲風。

B. A small town. 小鎮。

C. A television program about tornados.

關於龍捲風的電視節目。

* documentary〔ˌdɑkjə'mɛntərɪ〕 *n.* 紀錄片

tornado〔tɔr'nedo〕 *n.* 龍捲風

scary〔'skɛrɪ〕 *adj.* 可怕的；嚇人的

entire〔ɪn'taɪr〕 *adj.* 全部的；整個的

town〔taʊn〕 *n.* 城鎮　　**wipe out** 摧毀

powerful〔'paʊəfəl〕 *adj.* 強而有力的

warning〔'wɔrnɪŋ〕 *n.* 警告；警報

barely〔'bɛrlɪ〕 *adv.* 幾乎不　　shelter〔'ʃɛltə〕 *n.* 庇護所

mainly〔'menlɪ〕 *adv.* 主要地　　discuss〔dɪ'skʌs〕 *v.* 討論

program〔'progræm〕 *n.* 節目

24. (**A**) M : How much for these shoes?

男：這雙鞋多少錢？

W : They're only $2,800.

女：只要兩千八百元。

M：What! That's a rip-off!

男：什麼！根本就是敲竹槓。

Question：What does the man imply? 男士暗示什麼？

A. The price is too high. 價格太高。

B. The price is too low. 價格太低。

C. The jeans are damaged. 牛仔褲已受損。

* rip-off〔'rɪpˌɔf〕*n.* 敲竹槓；詐騙　　imply〔ɪm'plaɪ〕*v.* 暗示
jeans〔dʒinz〕*n. pl.* 牛仔褲
damage〔'dæmɪdʒ〕*v.* 損害

25. (**A**) M：What are you in the mood for tonight? Rice or noodles?

男：妳今晚想吃什麼？飯還是麵？

W：We've had noodles the last three nights.

女：我們連續三天晚上都吃麵了。

M：OK, then. Let's go to the Chinese place for fried rice.

男：好吧，我們去中式餐廳吃炒飯。

Question：What are the speakers discussing?

說話者在討論什麼？

A. What to eat tonight. 今天晚上吃什麼。

B. What they ate yesterday. 他們昨天吃了什麼。

C. What they will eat tomorrow. 他們明天要吃什麼。

* mood〔mud〕*n.* 心情　　***be in the mood for*** 有心情～
rice〔raɪs〕*n.* 米；米飯　　noodles〔'nudl̩z〕*n. pl.* 麵
Chinese〔tʃaɪ'niz〕*adj.* 中國的；中式的　　place〔ples〕*n.* 餐館
fried〔fraɪd〕*adj.* 油煎的；炒的；炸的　　***fried rice*** 炒飯

26. (**C**) M：This place is pretty bad. I'm not sure we should stay
here.

男：這地方真糟糕，我不確定我們是否該住在這裡。

W : What do you mean?

女：你這是什麼意思？

M : Well, the paint is peeling from the walls and the carpet is filthy.

男：嗯，牆壁的油漆在脫落，地毯也很髒。

Question : What are the speakers discussing?

說話者在討論什麼？

A. A restaurant. 餐廳。

B. A movie theatre. 電影院。

C. A hotel. 旅館。

＊ pretty〔'prɪtɪ〕*adv.* 相當；非常　　stay〔ste〕*v.* 停留；暫住
paint〔pent〕*n.* 油漆　　peel〔pil〕*v.*（皮、表面）剝落
carpet〔'kɑrpɪt〕*n.* 地毯　　filthy〔'fɪlθɪ〕*adj.* 骯髒的；污穢的
theater〔'θiətə〕*n.* 戲院；電影院
hotel〔ho'tɛl〕*n.* 飯店；旅館

27. (**C**) W : How's the weather is New York today?

女：紐約今天的天氣如何？

M : How should I know? I'm not a weatherman.

男：我怎麼知道？我又不是氣象播報員。

W : Oh, well, I just thought you might know since you were watching the news.

女：喔，好吧，我只是覺得你可能知道，因為你剛剛在看新聞。

Question : What is the man doing?

男士在做什麼？

A. Forecasting the weather. 播報氣象。

B. Reading a newspaper. 看報紙。

C. Watching television. 看電視。

* weather〔'wɛðə〕*n.* 天氣
  New York〔nju'jɔrk〕*n.* 紐約【美國東北部的一州】
  weatherman〔'wɛðə-mæn〕*n.* 氣象預報員
  since〔sɪns〕*conj.* 因為　　forecast〔for'kæst〕*v.* 預報（天氣）
  newspaper〔'nuz,pepə〕*n.* 報紙

28. (**C**) W：Where are you from?

女：你來自哪裡？

M：I'm originally from Taiwan but I lived in Tokyo for most of my life.

男：我原本來自台灣，但是我大多住在東京。

W：Wow, that's very interesting.

女：哇，真有趣。

Question：Where does the woman live now?

女士現在住哪裡？

A. Tokyo. 東京。　　　　　　B. Taiwan. 台灣。

C. It is impossible to say. 很難說。

* originally〔ə'rɪdʒənlɪ〕*adv.* 最初；原本
  Tokyo〔'tokɪ,o〕*n.* 東京【日本首都】
  interesting〔'ɪntrɪstɪŋ〕*adj.* 有趣的

29. (**A**) M：You have very pretty eyes. What color are they? Is that green?

男：妳有雙美麗的眼睛。是什麼顏色？綠色嗎？

W：They're actually brown, but I'm wearing blue contact lenses.

女：實際上是棕色，但是我戴了藍色的隱形眼鏡。

M：Oh, I see.

男：喔，原來是這樣。

Question : What color are the woman's eyes?

女士的眼睛是什麼顏色？

A. Brown. 棕色。

B. Blue. 藍色。

C. Green. 綠色。

* pretty〔'prɪtɪ〕*adj.* 美麗的　　color〔'kʌlɚ〕*n.* 顏色

actually〔'æktʃʊəlɪ〕*adv.* 事實上；實際上

brown〔braʊn〕*adj.* 棕色的　　contact〔'kɑntækt〕*n.* 接觸

lens〔lɛnz〕*n.* 鏡片　　***contact lenses*** 隱形眼鏡

I see. 我明白了；我知道了。

30. (**A**) M : Hi. I'm checking in for the nine-thirty flight to Los
Angeles.

男：嗨，我要辦理登機手續，九點三十分到洛杉磯的班機。

W : I'm sorry, sir, but that flight has already departed.

女：先生，很抱歉，但是那班飛機已經離開了。

M : Oh, no. Can you get me on another flight?

男：喔，不會吧。妳可以讓我上另一班飛機嗎？

Question : What has just happened? 剛剛發生了什麼事？

A. The man missed his flight. 男士錯過了他的班機。

B. The man went to Los Angeles. 男士去了洛杉磯。

C. The man checked in for his flight.

男士辦理了登機手續。

* ***check in*** 辦理登機手續　　flight〔flaɪt〕*n.* 班機

Los Angeles〔lɔs'ændʒələs〕*n.* 洛杉磯【美國加利福尼亞州西

南部一港市，簡稱 L.A.】

depart〔dɪ'pɑrt〕*v.* 出發；離開

miss〔mɪs〕*v.* 未趕上；錯過

國中會考英文聽力 ⑪

一、辨識句意

　　本部分共 10 題，每題有三個圖片選項，請聽光碟放音機播出的題目，聽後從試題冊上 A、B、C 圖片中，選出一個最適合的回答。每題播出二遍。

例：　（聽）　John enjoys taking a bath.
　　　（看）

　　　　(A)　　　　　　　(B)　　　　　　　(C)

正確答案為 C，請在答案紙上塗黑作答。

1.　　A.　　　　　　　B.　　　　　　　C.

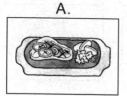　　

2.　　A.　　　　　　　B.　　　　　　　C.

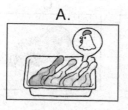　　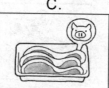

3.

A.   B.   C.

4.

A.   B.   C.

5.

A.   B.   C.

6.

A.   B.   C.

7.

A.   B.   C.

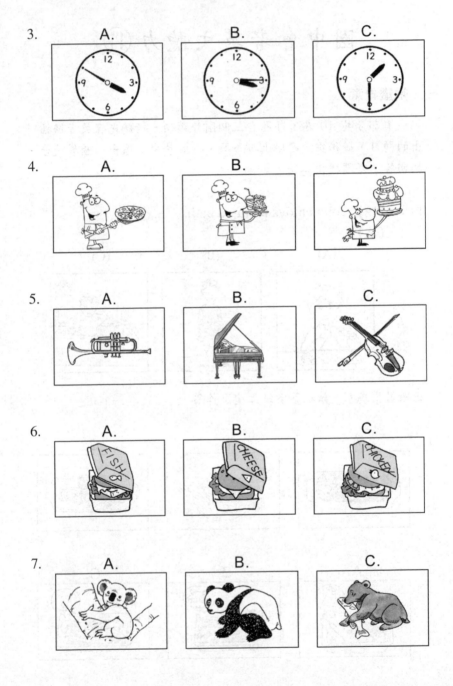

8.

9.

10.

二、基本問答：選出最適合的回答，完成對話。

本部份共 10 題，每題光碟放音機會播出一個問句或直述句，聽後從試題冊上 A、B、C 三個選項中，選出一個最適合的回答。每題播出二遍。

例： （聽） Hi, Mike. I haven't seen you for a long time. How are you doing?

（看） A. I'm watching TV.
B. I'm OK, thanks.
C. I'm at school.

正確答案為 B，請在答案紙上塗黑作答。

11. A. Black is the only color
     we have in exra-large.
    B. Sure, just bring a copy of
     the receipt.
    C. I'll check the storeroom.

12. A. I knew him back in junior
     high.
    B. I think it belongs to Ralph.
    C. Good luck finding it.

13. A. No, it's OK. Come on in.
    B. Take it easy next time.
    C. They always have a good
     time.

14. A. How about a beer?
    B. I don't drive during the
     week.
    C. I sure am.

15. A. No, I'm on vacation.
    B. No, get off at the next
     stop.
    C. Just a little bit will do.

16. A. We have all kinds.
    B. Sorry, not at this time.
    C. Try the other door.

17. A. The umbrella is behind
     the door.
    B. Sure. Let me know
     when you're free.
    C. You're going to get
     wet.

18. A. Oh sorry. I'll be quiet.
    B. It's great for long trips.
    C. I think we have a bad
     connection. Can you
     hear me now?

19. A. The river is that way.
    B. I can't drive.
    C. Let's wait for the bus.

20. A. My dog just died.
    B. Love is blind.
    C. The story is too funny.

三、言談理解（推論）

　　本部份共 10 題，每題光碟放音機會播出一段對話及一個相
關的問題，聽後從試題冊上 A、B、C 三個選項中，選出一個最
適合的回答。每題播出二遍。

例：（聽）(Man)　　May I help you?

　　　　(Woman)　Yes, I'd like to look at that red sweater.
　　　　　　　　　 How much is it?

　　　　(Man)　　It's one thousand dollars.

　　Question:　Where are the man and the woman?

（看）A. In a restaurant.

　　　B. In the living room.

　　　C. In a department store.

正確答案爲 C，請在答案紙上塗黑作答。

21. A. Six o'clock.
　　B. Earlier than everyone else.
　　C. As late as possible.

22. A. Both speakers enjoy coffee.
　　B. The café has great coffee.
　　C. The woman wants to be alone.

23. A. Talk to the woman.
　　B. Have lunch.
　　C. Save time.

24. A. She wants to wear the dress on Saturday.
　　B. The cleaners went out of business.
　　C. She will miss the party.

25. A. Scared.
　　B. Confused.
　　C. Embarrassed.

26. A. At the bus stop.
　　B. At school.
　　C. In Tainan.

27. A. Go to work.
　　B. Ask Dave for help.
　　C. Decorate the Christmas tree.

28. A. His parents are going out of town.
　　B. His parents will be in the parade.
　　C. His parents will be at work.

29. A. A type of chicken.
　　B. A breed of cattle.
　　C. A bird from Australia.

30. A. Mary hasn't called yet.
　　B. The weather is bad.
　　C. Mary isn't home yet.

國中會考英文聽力 ⑪ 詳解

一、辨識句意

1. (**B**) I'll have a garden salad, please. 我要田園沙拉，麻煩你。
   * garden (ˈgɑrdn̩) *n.* 花園；果園
   salad (ˈsæləd) *n.* 沙拉

2. (**A**) Tonight's special is fried chicken. 今晚的特餐是炸雞。
   * special (ˈspɛʃəl) *n.* (菜單上的) 特餐；特色菜
   fried (fraɪd) *adj.* 油炸的

3. (**C**) It's 1:30. 現在是一點三十分。

4. (**A**) Here's the pizza you ordered. 這是你點的披薩。
   * pizza (ˈpitsə) *n.* 披薩　　order (ˈɔrdɚ) *v.* 點 (菜)

5. (**A**) Trevor plays trumpet. 特雷弗吹小號。
   * trumpet (ˈtrʌmpɪt) *n.* 小喇叭；小號

6. (**B**) We had cheeseburgers for lunch. 我們午餐吃起司漢堡。
   * have (hæv) *v.* 吃；喝
   cheeseburger (ˈtʃiz,bɝgɚ) *n.* 起司漢堡

7. (**B**) We saw a panda at the zoo. 我們在動物園看到貓熊。
   * panda (ˈpændə) *n.* 貓熊　　zoo (zu) *n.* 動物園

8. (**B**) Be careful when using a knife. 用刀的時候要小心。
   * careful (ˈkɛrfəl) *adj.* 小心的　　use (juz) *v.* 使用
   knife (naɪf) *n.* 刀子

9. (**A**) There's something wrong with the toaster.
　　烤麵包機出了問題。

　　　* wrong〔rɔŋ〕*adj.* 故障的；情況不好的
　　　　toaster〔'tostɚ〕*n.* 烤麵包機

10. (**A**) Salvador is an artist. 薩爾瓦多是個藝術家。

　　　* artist〔'ɑrtɪst〕*n.* 藝術家；畫家

二、基本問答

11. (**C**) Do you have this shirt in a smaller size?
　　這件襯衫有小一點的尺寸嗎？

　　　A. Black is the only color we have in extra-large.
　　　　特大號的只有黑色。
　　　B. Sure, just bring a copy of the receipt.
　　　　當然，只要帶收據過來。
　　　C. I'll check the storeroom.　我看看倉庫。

　　　* shirt〔ʃɜt〕*n.* 襯衫　　size〔saɪz〕*n.* 尺寸
　　　　extra-large 特大號　　copy〔'kɑpɪ〕*n.* 一份
　　　　receipt〔rɪ'sit〕*n.* 收據
　　　　check〔tʃɛk〕*v.* 檢查；確認
　　　　storeroom〔'stor,rum〕*n.* 倉庫

12. (**B**) Who does that dog belong to? 那隻狗是誰的？

　　　A. I knew him back in junior high.
　　　　我在國中就認識他。
　　　B. I think it belongs to Ralph.　我想牠是拉夫的。
　　　C. Good luck finding it. 很幸運找到牠。

　　　* back〔bæk〕*adv.* 過去；從前；…以前　　*belong to* 屬於
　　　　good luck 運氣好

13. (**A**) Oh, I'm sorry. Did I catch you at a bad time?

喔，我很抱歉，我不該在這時候找你嗎？

A. No, it's OK. Come on in. 不，沒關係，請進。

B. Take it easy next time. 下次放輕鬆。

C. They always have a good time.

他們總是玩得很愉快。

* catch〔kætʃ〕v. 使措手不及；使驚慌失措

catch sb. at a bad time 使某人措手不及；來得不是時候

come on in 請進   ***take it easy*** 放輕鬆

have a good time 玩得愉快

14. (**A**) Hi, Joseph, come on in! What are you drinking?

嗨，喬瑟夫，請進！你在喝什麼？

A. How about a beer? 啤酒如何？

B. I don't drive during the week. 我這週不開車。

C. I sure am. 我的確是。

* ***How about~?*** ～如何？   beer〔bɪr〕n. 啤酒

drive〔draɪv〕v. 駕駛；開車

15. (**B**) I'd like to visit the zoo. Is this where I get off the bus?

我想要參觀動物園，我該在這邊下公車嗎？

A. No, I'm on vacation. 不，我在度假。

B. No, get off at the next stop. 不，在下一站下車。

C. Just a little bit will do. 一點點就夠了。

* ***would like to + V.*** 想要～   visit〔'vɪzɪt〕v. 參觀

zoo〔zu〕n. 動物園   ***get off*** 下（車）

vacation〔və'keʃən〕n. 假期   ***on vacation*** 度假中

stop〔stɑp〕n. 停車站   ***a little bit*** 一點點；少許

do〔du〕v. 行；可以；足夠

16. (**B**) I'm looking for a job. Are you hiring?

我正在找工作，你們有要雇用人嗎？

    A. We have all kinds. 我們所有的樣式都有。

    B. Sorry, not at this time. 抱歉，這時候沒有。

    C. Try the other door. 試看看另一扇門。

    * ***look for*** 尋找   hire〔haɪr〕*v.* 雇用

17. (**B**) Thanks for the offer, but not this time. Can I get a rain check? 謝謝你的提議，但這次不行。可以改期嗎？

    A. The umbrella is behind the door. 雨傘在門後面。

    B. Sure. Let me know when you're free.

        當然，你有空的時候跟我說。

    C. You're going to get wet. 你會淋濕。

    * offer〔'ɔfɚ〕*n.* 提議

      get a rain check 改天再說；改期

      umbrella〔ʌn'brɛlə〕*n.* 雨傘

      free〔fri〕*adj.* 有空的   wet〔wɛt〕*adj.* 濕的

18. (**C**) Could you please speak up? I can't hear you.

可以請你講大聲點嗎？我聽不到。

    A. Oh sorry. I'll be quiet. 喔，抱歉，我會安靜。

    B. It's great for long trips. 這很適合長途旅行。

    C. I think we have a bad connection. Can you hear me

        now? 我覺得是收訊不良，你現在聽得到嗎？

    * ***speak up*** 大聲說   quiet〔'kwaɪət〕*adj.* 安靜的

      great〔gret〕*adj.* 很棒的   trip〔trɪp〕*n.* 旅行

      connection〔kə'nɛkʃən〕*n.*（電話的）接線；通訊

      a bad connection 收訊不良

19. (**C**) Should we take a taxi or wait for the bus?
　　　　我們應該坐計程車還是等公車？

　　A. The river is that way. 河流是那個方向。

　　B. I can't drive. 我不會開車。

　　C. Let's wait for the bus. 一起等公車吧。

　　* taxi〔'tæksɪ〕*n.* 計程車　　　***wait for*** 等待
　　　river〔'rɪvɚ〕*n.* 河流　　　way〔we〕*n.* 方向
　　　drive〔draɪv〕*v.* 開車　　　***let's + V.*** 讓我們來～；一起～。

20. (**A**) Eddie, what's wrong? What are you crying about?
　　　　艾迪，怎麼了？你為什麼哭？

　　A. My dog just died. 我的狗剛剛死了。

　　B. Love is blind. 愛情是盲目的。

　　C. The story is too funny. 這故事太好笑了。

　　* ***What's wrong?*** 怎麼了？
　　　blind〔blaɪnd〕*adj.* 看不見的；盲目的
　　　Love is blind.【諺】愛情是盲目的。
　　　funny〔'fʌnɪ〕*adj.* 滑稽的；好笑的

三、言談理解

21. (**A**) M：What time do you get up in the morning?
　　　　男：妳早上幾點起床？

　　W：I get up around six o'clock.
　　　　女：我大概六點起床。

　　M：Why so early? I try to sleep as late as possible.
　　　　男：為什麼這麼早？我都盡可能睡晚一點。

　　Question：What time does the woman get up in the
　　　　　　　morning? 女士早上幾點起床？

A. Six o'clock. 六點。

B. Earlier than everyone else. 比其他人都早。

C. As late as possible. 盡可能晚一點。

* **get up** 起床　　**as ~ as possible** 盡可能~

22. (**C**) W：Where can I get a good cup of coffee around here?

女：在這裡附近哪裡可以買到一杯好咖啡？

M：There's a café at the corner. They have great coffee.

男：轉角有間咖啡店，他們的咖啡很棒。

W：Would you like to join me?

女：你要跟我一起去嗎？

Question：Which of the following statements is NOT true?

下列敘述何者「不」是真的？

A. Both speakers enjoy coffee.

兩個說話者都喜愛咖啡。

B. The café has great coffee.

那家咖啡店有很好的咖啡。

C. The woman wants to be alone.

女士想要獨自一個人。

* coffee〔ˈkɔfɪ〕*n.* 咖啡　　café〔kəˈfe〕*n.* 咖啡店

corner〔ˈkɔrnɚ〕*n.* 轉角處；街角

join〔dʒɔɪn〕*v.* 加入　　statement〔ˈstetmənt〕*n.* 敘述

alone〔əˈlon〕*adj.* 獨自的；單獨的

23. (**A**) M：Hey Moira, do you have a minute?

男：嘿，莫拉，妳有空嗎？

W：I'm really kind of busy, Dexter. Can it wait? 【詳見背景說明】

女：我真的有點忙，德克斯特。能等一下嗎？

M : No problem. It's nothing urgent. I'll come back and
   see you after lunch.

男：沒問題，不是緊急的事。我等一下過來，午餐後見。

Question : What does the man want to do? 男士想做什麼？

A. Talk to the woman. 跟女士講話。

B. Have lunch. 吃午餐。

C. Save time. 節省時間。

* minute〔'mɪnɪt〕*n.* 一會兒；片刻
  have a minute 有空   ***kind of*** 有一點
  urgent〔'ɝdʒənt〕*adj.* 緊急的；迫切的
  have〔hæv〕*v.* 吃；喝   save〔sev〕*v.* 節省

24. (**A**) W : Did you take my dress to the cleaners this afternoon?

女：你今天下午有把我的洋裝拿去洗衣店嗎？

M : Yes, it will be ready next Tuesday.

男：有，下週二會洗好。

W : Oh, no! The party is on Saturday!

女：喔，不！派對是在週六！

Question : What does the woman imply? 女士暗示什麼？

A. She wants to wear the dress on Saturday.
    她週六要穿那洋裝。

B. The cleaners went out of business.
    洗衣店結束營業了。

C. She will miss the party. 她會錯過派對。

* dress〔drɛs〕*n.* 洋裝
  the cleaners 洗衣店；乾洗店
  imply〔ɪm'plaɪ〕*v.* 暗示
  out of business 結束營業；倒閉   miss〔mɪs〕*v.* 錯過

25. (**C**) M : How was the game yesterday?

男：昨天的比賽如何？

W : Awful. We lost. They murdered us. It was embarrassing. 【詳見背景說明】

女：糟透了，我們輸了。他們徹底擊敗我們，實在很尷尬。

M : Keep your chin up. You'll get them next time.

男：打起精神，你們下次會擊垮他們。

Question : How does the woman feel about the game?

女士對於比賽有何感想？

A. Scared. 害怕的。

B. Confused. 困惑的。

C. Embarrassed. 尷尬的。

* game〔gem〕*n.* 比賽
  awful〔'ɔfʊl〕*n.*（失敗、感冒等）很糟的
  murder〔'mɝdɚ〕*v.* 徹底擊敗
  embarrassing〔ɪm'bærəsɪŋ〕*adj.* 令人尷尬的
  chin〔tʃɪn〕*n.* 下巴
  keep one's chin up 打起精神；不要氣餒
  get〔gɛt〕*v.*（比賽）擊垮　　scared〔skɛrd〕*adj.* 害怕的
  confused〔kən'fjuzd〕*adj.* 困惑的
  embarrassed〔ɪm'bærəst〕*adj.* 尷尬的

26. (**C**) W : Is that your sister standing at the bus stop?

女：站在公車站的那位是你妹妹嗎？

M : No, it can't be. She's visiting our grandmother in Tainan.

男：不，不可能，她去台南探望我們的祖母。

W : Wow, it sure looks like her.

女：哇，看起來真像她。

Question: Where is the man's sister? 男士的妹妹在哪裡？

A. At the bus stop. 在公車站。

B. At school. 在學校。

C. In Tainan. 在台南。

* stop〔stɑp〕*n.* 停車站
grandmother〔'grænd,mʌðɚ〕*n.* 祖母；奶奶

27. (**C**) M：What are these flowers for?

男：這些花是做什麼用的？

W：We're going to use them to decorate the Christmas tree. Would you mind giving me a hand?

女：我們要用這些花來裝飾聖誕樹，你介意幫我個忙嗎？

M：Sorry, I'm going to work in ten minutes. Maybe Dave can help you.

男：抱歉，我十分鐘後要去工作，或許戴夫可以幫妳。

Question：What does the woman want to do?

女士要做什麼？

A. Go to work. 去工作。

B. Ask Dave for help. 要求戴夫幫忙。

C. Decorate the Christmas tree. 布置聖誕樹。

* decorate〔'dɛkə,ret〕*v.* 裝飾
Christmas tree 聖誕樹　　mind〔maɪnd〕*v.* 介意
Would you mind + V-ing? 你介意～；請你～好嗎？
give sb. a hand 幫某人的忙　　***ask sb. for help*** 請某人幫忙

28. (**A**) W：Hi, Oliver. Are you coming to the parade with us tomorrow?

女：嗨，奧利佛，你明天要不要跟我們一起去遊行？

M：I'd love to, but I have to babysit my little brother.
My parents are going out of town for the weekend.

男：我很想去，但是我得當保姆照顧我弟弟。我父母這週末要到外地去。

W：Why don't you bring him along? We can take turns watching him.

女：你何不帶他一起過來？我們可以輪流照顧他。

Question：Why is Oliver babysitting his little brother?
　　　　奧利佛為何要當保姆照顧他弟弟？

A. His parents are going out of town. 他的父母要去外地。
B. His parents will be in the parade. 他的父母會去遊行。
C. His parents will be at work. 他的父母要工作。

* parade〔pə'red〕*n.* 遊行
would love to + V. 很想要～
babysit〔'bebɪ,sɪt〕*v.* 當（臨時）保姆照顧～
out of town 出城；到外地
bring *sb.* ***along*** 帶某人過來
take turns + V-ing 輪流～
watch〔wɑtʃ〕*v.* 看護；照顧　　***at work*** 在工作

29. (**C**) M：Are you ready to order?

男：準備好要點餐了嗎？

W：Yes, but…I have a question. What's "ostrich"?

女：好的，但是…我有個問題，什麼是"ostrich"？

M：Oh, it's a bird from Australia. It tastes a bit like chicken. You should try it. It's very tasty.

男：喔，那是種來自澳洲的鳥類，吃起來像雞肉。妳應該嘗試看看，很好吃。

Question : What is an ostrich?

　　　　什麼是"ostrich"?

A. A type of chicken. 一種雞肉。

B. A breed of cattle. 一種牛。

C. A bird from Australia. <u>一種來自澳洲的鳥類。</u>

*order〔'ɔrdɚ〕v. 點（菜）　　ostrich〔'ɔstrɪtʃ〕n. 鴕鳥
　Australia〔ɔ'streljə〕n. 澳洲　　taste〔test〕v. 嚐起來
　chicken〔'tʃɪkɪn〕n. 雞肉
　tasty〔'testɪ〕adj. 好吃的；美味的
　breed〔brid〕n. 品種　　cattle〔'kætl̩〕n. 牛

30. (**A**) M : Have you heard from Mary yet?

　　　男：妳有瑪麗的消息嗎？

　　　W : She said she'd call when they arrive at the airport.

　　　女：她說他們到了機場會打電話。

　　　M : It's getting late. I hope they're all right.

　　　男：時間很晚了，希望他們沒事。

　　　Question : Why is the man worried?

　　　　　　　男士為何擔心？

　　　A. Mary hasn't called yet. <u>瑪麗還沒打電話。</u>

　　　B. The weather is bad. 天氣不好。

　　　C. Mary isn't home yet. 瑪麗還沒到家。

　　　*hear from 收到…的信；得知…的消息
　　　 arrive〔ə'raɪv〕v. 到達
　　　 airport〔'ɛr͵port〕n. 機場
　　　 all right 平安；一切順利　　not…yet 尚未…
　　　 worried〔'wɝɪd〕adj. 擔心的

國中會考英文聽力 ⑫

一、辨識句意

　　本部分共 10 題，每題有三個圖片選項，請聽光碟放音機播出的題目，聽後從試題冊上 A、B、C 圖片中，選出一個最適合的回答。每題播出二遍。

例：　（聽）　John enjoys taking a bath.
　　　（看）

(A) 　　(B) 　　(C)

正確答案為 C，請在答案紙上塗黑作答。

1.　A. 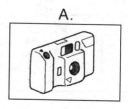　　B. 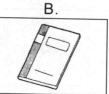　　C.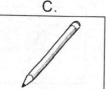

2.　A. 　　B. 　　C.

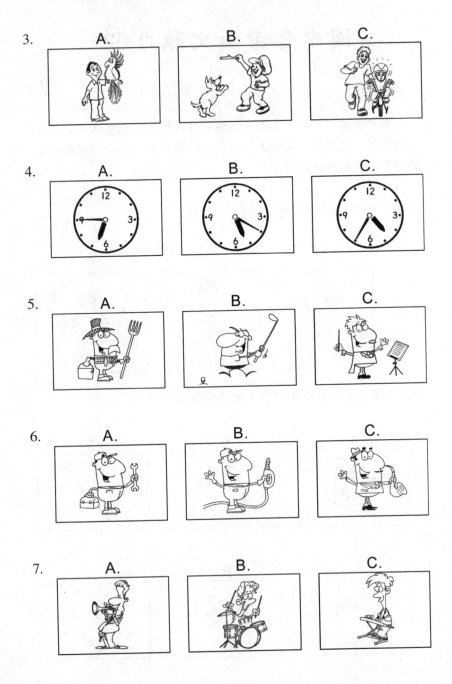

8.　A.　　　　B.　　　　C.

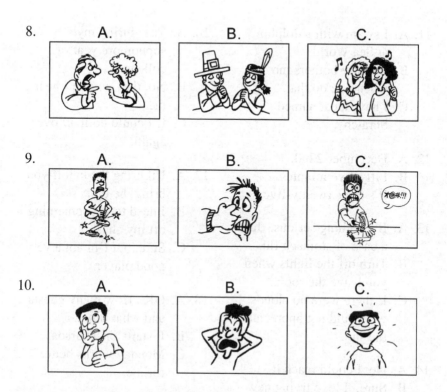

9.　A.　　　　B.　　　　C.

10.　A.　　　　B.　　　　C.

二、基本問答：選出最適合的回答，完成對話。

　　　本部份共 10 題，每題光碟放音機會播出一個問句或直述句，聽後從試題冊上 A、B、C 三個選項中，選出一個最適合的回答。每題播出二遍。

例：　（聽）　Hi, Mike. I haven't seen you for a long time.
　　　　　　　How are you doing?

　　　（看）　A. I'm watching TV.
　　　　　　　B. I'm OK, thanks.
　　　　　　　C. I'm at school.

　　　正確答案為 B，請在答案紙上塗黑作答。

11. A. I swam with a dolphin
at Sea World.
B. It really bothers me
when you do that.
C. I have a cat named
Scratchy.

12. A. December 22nd.
B. Fifty-five minutes.
C. It's three twenty-five.

13. A. It's nothing serious. Just
a case of stomach flu.
B. Turn off the lights when
you leave the room.
C. If there were no clouds,
we would not appreciate
the sun.

14. A. No, I could reach it.
B. Sure. I love trying new
things.
C. I've never been to Hong
Kong.

15. A. I haven't had a chance
to see him.
B. Like a fish out of water.
C. I couldn't be happier
with it.

16. A. Yes, during my
sophomore year of
college.
B. No, they couldn't hear
me.
C. If I could do it all over
again.

17. A. I'll bring the ball if you
bring the bat.
B. I need to get something
off my chest.
C. Sure, but I'm not a very
good player.

18. A. OK. How many guests
and what time?
B. It starts on Thursday.
C. Monday works better
for me.

19. A. I'm out of shape.
B. I'm an accountant.
C. Computer science.

20. A. We close at midnight.
B. Sure, all you can find.
C. Sorry, cash only.

三、言談理解（推論）

　　本部份共 10 題，每題光碟放音機會播出一段對話及一個相
關的問題，聽後從試題冊上 A、B、C 三個選項中，選出一個最
適合的回答。每題播出二遍。

例： （聽） (Man)　　May I help you?

　　　　　 (Woman)　Yes, I'd like to look at that red sweater.
　　　　　　　　　 How much is it?

　　　　　 (Man)　　It's one thousand dollars.

　　　　 Question: Where are the man and the woman?

（看）　A. In a restaurant.

　　　 B. In the living room.

　　　 C. In a department store.

正確答案為 C，請在答案紙上塗黑作答。

21. A. Advice.
　　B. Flowers.
　　C. Candy.

22. A. He's a good worker.
　　B. He's been late before.
　　C. He's out of excuses.

23. A. A computer crash.
　　B. A car crash.
　　C. A plane crash.

24. A. The salt.
　　B. Health advice.
　　C. Heart disease.

25. A. Strawberries are out of
　　　 season.
　　B. Strawberries are grown
　　　 in warm places.
　　C. South America is too hot.

26. A. She thinks it's cute.
　　B. She doesn't like Jerry's
　　　 tattoo.
　　C. She wants to get one,
　　　 too.

27. A. Boston.
　　B. Detroit.
　　C. Cincinnati.

28. A. Siblings.
　　B. Co-workers.
　　C. Husband and wife.

29. A. Plans for the weekend.
　　B. Plans for the holiday.
　　C. Plans for the evening.

30. A. The kid is a professional.
　　B. The kid isn't very good.
　　C. The kid is a teacher.

國中會考英文聽力 ⑫ 詳解

一、辨識句意

1. (**C**) May I borrow your pencil? 我可以跟你借支鉛筆嗎？
    * borrow〔'baro〕v. 借（入）　　pencil〔'pɛnsl̩〕n. 鉛筆

2. (**B**) Koko is wearing a headband. 可可正戴著頭巾。
    * wear〔wɛr〕v. 穿；戴　　headband〔'hɛd,bænd〕n. 頭巾；頭帶

3. (**B**) Mr. Wang's dog can perform tricks. 王先生的狗會表演特技。
    * perform〔pɚ'fɔrm〕v. 表演；做　　trick〔trɪk〕n. 特技

4. (**B**) It's 5:20. 現在是五點二十分。

5. (**B**) Charles enjoys golfing. 查爾斯喜歡打高爾夫球。
    * *enjoy + V-ing* 喜愛～　　golf〔gɔlf〕v. 打高爾夫球

6. (**C**) Pedro is a musician. 皮特爾是個音樂家。
    * musician〔mju'zɪʃən〕n. 音樂家

7. (**B**) Quincy plays the drums. 昆西打鼓。
    * drum〔drʌm〕n. 鼓

8. (**A**) Mr. and Ms. Chou are having an argument.
    周先生和周小姐在吵架。
    * argument〔'argjəmənt〕n. 爭論
      have an argument 爭論；爭吵

9. (**B**) Jimmy punched Johnny in the nose. 吉米用拳頭打強尼的鼻子。
    * punch〔pʌntʃ〕v. 用拳猛擊　　nose〔noz〕n. 鼻子

10. (**C**) Myron is very pleased.　米倫很高興。

    * pleased〔plizd〕*adj.* 高興的

二、基本問答

11. (**C**) Bobby just got a puppy.　It's so cute!　Do you have any
pets?　巴比最近養了一隻小狗，好可愛！你有養寵物嗎？

    A.　I swam with a dolphin at Sea World.
　　　我在海洋世界跟海豚一起游泳。

    B.　It really bothers me when you do that.
　　　你那麼做真的讓我很困擾。

    C.　I have a cat named Scratchy.　<u>我有一隻貓叫抓抓。</u>

    * puppy〔ˋpʌpɪ〕*n.*（未滿一歲的）小狗
    pet〔pɛt〕*n.* 寵物
    swim〔swɪm〕*v.* 游泳【三態為 swim-swam-swum】
    bother〔ˋbɑðɚ〕*v.* 困擾　　name〔nem〕*v.* 給…命名
    scratchy〔ˋskrætʃɪ〕*adj.* 沙沙作響的；讓人發癢的

12. (**C**) My watch has stopped.　Could you please tell me the time?
我的手錶停了，可以請你告訴我現在幾點嗎？

    A.　December 22nd.　十二月二十二日。

    B.　Fifty-five minutes.　五十五分鐘。

    C.　It's three twenty-five.　<u>現在是三點二十五分。</u>

    * watch〔watʃ〕*n.* 手錶　　***the time*** 時間；…時…分

13. (**A**) What did the doctor say?　醫生說了什麼？

    A.　It's nothing serious.　Just a case of stomach flu.
　　　<u>不嚴重，只是急性腸胃炎。</u>

    B.　Turn off the lights when you leave the room.
　　　離開房間時把燈關掉。

C. If there were no clouds, we would not appreciate the sun.
如果沒有雲，我們就不覺得陽光可愛。(比喻逆境讓成功顯得
更可貴。)

* serious (ˈsɪrɪəs) *adj.* 嚴重的　　stomach (ˈstʌmək) *n.* 胃
flu (flu) *n.* 流行性感冒　***stomach flu*** 急性腸胃炎
turn off 關掉 (燈、電器)　　light (laɪt) *n.* 燈
cloud (klaʊd) *n.* 雲　　appreciate (əˈpriʃɪˌet) *v.* 欣賞

14. (**B**) Hi, Pablo. I bought this candy in Hong Kong. Would you
like to try some?
嗨，巴勃羅，我在香港買了這個糖果，你要吃看看嗎？

A. No, I could reach it. 不，我拿得到。

B. Sure. I love trying new things.
好啊，我喜歡嘗試新東西。

C. I've never been to Hong Kong. 我沒去過香港。

* candy (ˈkændɪ) *n.* 糖果　***Hong Kong*** 香港
reach (ritʃ) *v.* (伸手) 取得　***have been to*** 去過

15. (**C**) Oh, you've got a new laptop. How do you like it?
喔，你買了新筆電，你覺得如何？

A. I haven't had a chance to see him. 我沒機會看到他。

B. Like a fish out of water. 渾身不自在。

C. I couldn't be happier with it. 有了它再高興不過了。

* laptop (ˈlæpˌtɑp) *n.* 筆記型電腦
How do you like ~? 你覺得～如何？
chance (tʃæns) *n.* 機會
like a fish out of water 渾身不自在
couldn't be + 形容詞比較級　再⋯不過了；非常

16. (**A**) Didn't you live in Tokyo for a year? 你不是在東京住了一年？

A. Yes, during my sophomore year of college.
　　是的，在我大二的時候。

B. No, they couldn't hear me. 不，他們聽不到我的聲音。

C. If I could do it all over again. 如果我能重新再來一次。

* Tokyo〔'tokɪ,o〕*n.* 東京【日本首都】
sophomore〔'sɑfm̩,or〕*n.* (四年制大學)二年級學生
college〔'kɑlɪdʒ〕*n.* 大學　　***over again*** 重新

17. (**C**) Care to join me for a game of tennis?
　　想和我打一場網球賽嗎？

　　A. I'll bring the ball if you bring the bat.
　　　如果你帶球棒，我就帶球。

　　B. I need to get something off my chest.
　　　我需要傾吐些心事。

　　C. Sure, but I'm not a very good player.
　　　好啊，但我打得不是很好。

　　* ***care to V.*** 想要…
　　　join〔dʒɔɪn〕*v.* 加入；和(某人)一起做同樣的事
　　　tennis〔'tɛnɪs〕*n.* 網球　　bat〔bæt〕*n.* 球棒
　　　chest〔tʃɛst〕*n.* 內心；胸腔
　　　get something off *one's* ***chest*** 傾吐心事

18. (**A**) Hi, I'd like to make a reservation for Friday night.
　　嗨，我想要預約週五晚上。

　　A. OK. How many guests and what time?
　　　好的，有多少客人，幾點呢？

　　B. It starts on Thursday. 週四開始。

　　C. Monday works better for me.【詳見背景說明】
　　　對我而言週一比較好。

　　* ***would like to + V.*** 想要~　　reservation〔,rɛzə'veʃən〕*n.* 預約
　　　make a reservation 預約　　guest〔gɛst〕*n.* 客人
　　　work〔wɜk〕*v.* 行得通

19. (**C**) Donald tells me that you go to Stanford. What is your major? 唐納德告訴我你就讀史丹佛，你主修什麼？

    A. I'm out of shape. 我身體不好。

    B. I'm an accountant. 我是個會計師。

    C. Computer science. <u>電腦科學。</u>

    * ***go to*** 上（大學）

    Standford〔ˈstænfəd〕*n.* 史丹佛大學【位於美國加州】

    major〔ˈmedʒə〕*n.* 主修科目   ***out of shape*** 身體狀況不佳

    accountant〔əˈkaʊntənt〕*n.* 會計師

20. (**C**) I'm afraid I don't have enough cash on me. Do you accept credit cards?

    我恐怕身上沒有足夠的現金，你們接受信用卡嗎？

    A. We close at midnight. 我們半夜關門。

    B. Sure, all you can eat. 當然，吃到飽。

    C. Sorry, cash only. <u>抱歉，只收現金。</u>

    * afraid〔əˈfred〕*adj.*（表示遺憾）恐怕…

    cash〔kæʃ〕*n.* 現金   accept〔əkˈsɛpt〕*v.* 接受

    credit card 信用卡   midnight〔ˈmɪdˌnaɪt〕*n.* 半夜

三、言談理解

21. (**C**) M：Thank you for the gift. It was very thoughtful of you.

    男：謝謝妳的禮物，妳真體貼。

    W：You're welcome. I hope you like it.

    女：不客氣，希望你喜歡。

    M：Of course! I love chocolate.

    男：當然！我愛巧克力。

    Question：What did the woman give the man?

        女士給男士什麼？

A. Advice. 建議。   B. Flowers. 花。

C. Candy. 糖果。

* gift〔gɪft〕*n.* 禮物
  thoughtful〔'θɔtfəl〕*adj.* 體貼的
  of course 當然   chocolate〔'tʃɔklɪt〕*n.* 巧克力
  advice〔əd'vaɪs〕*n.* 忠告；勸告

22. (**B**) W：You're late again, Tom, for the third time this week.

    女：你又遲到了，湯姆。這是你本週第三次遲到。

    M：I know. I'm sorry. It's just that—.

    男：我知道，很抱歉，就是那個—。

    W：I don't want to hear any more excuses. Get here on time or else.

    女：我不想要聽到任何藉口，就是準時到這，否則承擔一切後果。

    Question：What do we know about the man?

        關於男士，我們可以得知什麼？

    A. He's a good worker. 他是個好員工。

    B. He's been late before. 他之前遲到過。

    C. He's out of excuses. 他沒有藉口了。

    * excuse〔ɪk'skjus〕*n.* 藉口   *on time* 準時
    or else （表示警告或威脅）否則將承擔一切後果
    worker〔'wɝkɚ〕*n.* 員工
    be out of excuses 用完藉口

23. (**C**) M：Did you see the news today? A plane crashed in Hawaii.

    男：妳有看今天的新聞嗎？一架飛機在夏威夷失事了。

    W：That's terrible. Were there any survivors?

    女：真可怕，有任何生還者嗎？

M：None.

男：一個都沒有。

Question：What happened in Hawaii?

在夏威夷發生了什麼事？

A. A computer crash. 電腦當機。

B. A car crash. 車禍。

C. A plane crash. 飛機失事。

＊crash〔kræʃ〕*n. v.*（飛機）墜毀；失事；（電腦）當機
Hawaii〔hə'waɪjə〕*n.* 夏威夷州【美國的一州，由夏威夷群島所構成】
plane crash 墜機；飛機失事
terrible〔'tɛrəbl̩〕*adj.* 可怕的
survivor〔sə'vaɪvə〕*n.* 生還者
computer crash 電腦當機　　***car crash*** 車禍

24. (**A**) M：Would you please pass the salt?

男：可以請妳把鹽傳給我嗎？

W：You know, too much salt in one's diet can lead to heart disease.

女：你知道的，飲食中鹽分太多會導致心臟病。

M：I didn't ask for health advice. I asked for the salt.

男：我不是要求健康方面的建議，我是要鹽。

Question：What did the man ask for? 男士要什麼？

A. The salt. 鹽。

B. Health advice. 健康方面的建議。

C. Heart disease. 心臟病。

＊pass〔pæs〕*v.* 傳遞　　salt〔sɔlt〕*n.* 鹽
diet〔'daɪət〕*n.* 飲食　　***lead to*** 導致
heart〔hɑrt〕*n.* 心臟　　disease〔dɪ'ziz〕*n.* 疾病
health〔hɛlθ〕*n.* 健康　　advice〔əd'vaɪs〕*n.* 忠告；建議

25. (**B**) M : These strawberries are delicious!

男：這些草莓好好吃！

W : Yes, I wonder where they came from. They're not in season right now.

女：對呀，我在想它們來自何處。現在不是盛產季節。

M : Probably somewhere warm, like South America.

男：或許是某個溫暖的地方，像是南美洲。

Question : What does the man imply? 男士暗示什麼？

A. Strawberries are out of season. 草莓現在非盛產。

B. Strawberries are grown in warm places.

　　草莓種植在溫暖的地方。

C. South America is too hot. 南美洲太熱。

* strawberry〔'strɔ͵bɛrɪ〕*n.* 草莓

delicious〔dɪ'lɪʃəs〕*adj.* 好吃的；美味的

wonder〔'wʌndɚ〕*v.* 想知道　　season〔'sizn̩〕*n.* 季節

in season （蔬菜、水果）當季的；盛產的

probably〔'prɑbəblɪ〕*adv.* 可能

South America 南美洲　　imply〔ɪm'plaɪ〕*v.* 暗示

out of season 非盛產的；不合時令的

grow〔gro〕*v.* 種植；栽培

26. (**B**) M : What do you think of Jerry's new tattoo?

男：妳覺得傑瑞的新刺青如何？

W : Well, my mother always told me, if you can't say anything nice, don't say anything at all.

女：嗯，我媽總是跟我說，如果你無法說好話，那就什麼都不要說。

M : I know what you mean. I would never get a tattoo.

男：我知道妳的意思，我永遠不會刺青。

Question : What does the woman imply?

女士暗示什麼？

A. She thinks it's cute. 她覺得刺青很可愛。

B. She doesn't like Jerry's tattoo. 她不喜歡傑瑞的刺青。

C. She wants to get one, too. 她也想有個刺青。

* ***What do you think of~?*** 你認為～怎麼樣？
  tattoo〔tæ'tu〕*n.* 刺青　　***not…at all*** 一點也不…

27. (**A**) W : So, where are you from?

女：那麼你是來自哪裡？

M : Detroit. And you?

男：底特律，妳呢？

W : Cincinnati. What brings you to Boston?

女：辛辛那提，什麼事讓你來到波士頓的？

Question : Where is this conversation taking place?

這對話是在哪裡發生的？

A. Boston. 波士頓。

B. Detroit. 底特律。

C. Cincinnati. 辛辛那提。

* Detroit〔dɪ'trɔɪt〕*n.* 底特律【位於美國密西根州（Michigan）的
  工業城市，以汽車工業聞名】
  Cincinnati〔ˌsɪnsə'nætɪ〕*n.* 辛辛那提【美國俄亥俄州（Ohio）
  西南部的城市】
  bring A ***to*** B　使 A 到達 B
  Boston〔'bɔstn̩〕*n.* 波士頓【美國麻薩諸塞州（Massachusetts）
  的首都】

28. (**B**) M : Did you speak with Mr. Gibson about our proposal?

男：妳跟吉勃遜先生講過我們的提案了嗎？

W : Yes, I did. He likes our idea but wants to think it over before he makes a decision.

女：有，我講了。他很喜歡我們的想法，但是他想在做決定之前再考慮一下。

M : I hope he says yes. It will make our jobs that much easier.

男：我希望他說好，這會讓我們的工作容易許多。

Question : What is most likely the relationship between the speakers? 說話者最可能是什麼關係？

A. Siblings. 兄弟姊妹。

B. Co-workers. 同事。

C. Husband and wife. 夫妻。

* proposal〔prə'pozḷ〕*n.* 提案；計畫
   think over 仔細考慮   decision〔dɪ'sɪʒən〕*n.* 決定
   make a decision 做決定
   relationship〔rɪ'leʃən‚ʃɪp〕*n.* 關係
   siblings〔'sɪblɪŋz〕*n. pl.* 兄弟姊妹
   co-worker〔'ko‚wɝkɚ〕*n.* 同事

29. (**C**) W : What do you feel like doing tonight?

女：你今晚想做什麼？

M : I don't feel like doing much. I'm exhausted.

男：我不太想做什麼事情，我覺得很累。

W : How about we stay home, order a pizza and rent a movie?

女：那我們待在家，訂披薩，然後租個電影來看如何？

Question : What are the speakers discussing?
      說話者在討論什麼？

A. Plans for the weekend. 週末的計畫。

B. Plans for the holiday. 假日的計畫。

C. Plans for the evening. 晚上的計畫。

* *feeling like* + *V-ing* 想要～

　exhausted〔 ɪgˋzɔstɪd 〕*adj.* 筋疲力盡的

　order〔ˋɔrdɚ〕*v.* 訂購　　pizza〔ˋpitsə〕*n.* 披薩

　rent〔 rɛnt 〕*v.* 租　　discuss〔 dɪˋskʌs 〕*v.* 討論

　plan〔 plæn 〕*n.* 計畫

　weekend〔ˋwikˋɛnd〕*n.* 週末

30. (**B**) W：Where is that noise coming from?

　　　　 女：那噪音是從哪裡來的？

　　　　 M：It's the kid next door. He's taken up the violin.

　　　　 男：是隔壁的小孩，他開始學拉小提琴。

　　　　 W：Sounds like he needs more lessons.

　　　　 女：聽起來他需要多上點課。

　　　　 Question：What does the woman imply?

　　　　　　　　 女士暗示什麼？

　　　　 A. The kid is a professional. 那小孩很專業。

　　　　 B. The kid isn't very good. 那小孩不太熟練。

　　　　 C. The kid is a teacher. 那小孩是老師。

* noise〔 nɔɪz 〕*n.* 噪音　　kid〔 kɪd 〕*n.* 小孩

　 next foor 隔壁　　 *take up* 開始從事

　violin〔ˏvaɪəˋlɪn〕*n.* 小提琴

　 sound like 聽起來似乎

　lesson〔ˋlɛsn̩〕*n.* 課程

　professional〔 prəˋfɛʃənl̩ 〕*adj.* 專業的

　good〔 gʊd 〕*adj.* 熟練的；擅長的

背景說明

　　本書有許多美國人常用的口語，非常生活化且實用，
特地總結在這裡說明，以供參考。(回-頁數-題)

1. ***Be a sport.*** (2-9-18)

　　sport 主要是作「運動」解，可當「愛好運動的人」，引
申為「有運動家精神的人；堂正大度的人；熱於助人的夥伴；
重友情的人」，如：***Be a sport***, and lend me a hand. (講點
交情，助我一臂之力吧。)【詳見「東華英漢大辭典」p.3342】

　　Be a sport.
　　= Be nice.
　　= Be a good friend.

2. ***Have a heart.*** (2-9-18)

　　have a heart 字面意思是「有一顆心」，引申為「發發
慈悲；行行好吧。」

　　Have a heart.
　　= Be generous.
　　= Be sympathetic to others.

　　　generous (ˈdʒɛnərəs) *adj.* 慷慨的；大方的
　　　sympathetic (ˌsɪmpəˈθɛtɪk) *adj.* 有同情心的

3. ***Good thing we have a spare.*** (2-10-21)

　　這句話的意思是「幸好我們有備胎。」Good thing 是 It's
a good thing (that) 的簡化，意思是「幸好…」。

　　Good thing (***that***)…
　　= It's a good thing (that)…
　　= It is fortunate for us (that)…

　　　fortunate (ˈfɔrtʃənɪt) *adj.* 幸運的

4. *School gets out at 3:00.* (3-7-11)

　　這句話的意思是「學校三點放學。」School gets out. 是慣用語，表示「學校放學（下課）。」

School gets out at 3:00.
= School lets out at 3:00.
= Class is dismissed at 3:00.

　　　let out　（學校、集會）終了；解散
　　　dismiss〔dɪs'mɪs〕*v.* 解散；下（課）

5. *Yes, he said he's stuck in traffic.* (3-8-13)

　　這句話的意思是「有，他說他遇到塞車。」

He's stuck in traffic.
= He is detained by traffic.
= He is delayed by traffic.

　　　　　detain〔dɪ'ten〕*v.* 使耽誤　　delay〔dɪ'le〕*v.* 使延遲

6. *Way after midnight.* (4-9-16)

　　這句話的意思是「午夜之後很久」(= *very late, long after 12:00 a.m.*)。這裡的 way 是用來強調 after。

7. *You don't hear about those every day, do you?* (4-12-23)

　　這句話的意思是「你不會天天聽到這樣的事，不是嗎？」也可說成：This is not a common occurrence.（那不是常見的事情。）【common〔'kɑmən〕*adj.* 常見的 occurrence〔ə'kɝəns〕*n.* 發生的事；事件】

8. *Give it some room.* (5-7-12)

　　這裡的 room 是作「空間」(= *space*) 解，所以這句話字面上的意思是「給它一些空間」，就是「離它遠一點」(= *back away from the object*)。也常說成：Give me

some room.（= *Give me some space to move around.*）
意思是「給我一點空間。」因為美國人彼此不會靠很近，
喜歡有自己的空間。

9. *I'm not from around here.* (5-9-17)

　　這句話的字面的意思是「我不是來自於這裡附近。」
也就是「我不住這附近；我只是路過。」

　　I'm not from around here.
　　= I don't live here.
　　= I am just passing through.

10. *Put it down before someone gets hurt.* (5-10-20)

　　這句話的意思是「在還沒有人受傷之前收手吧。」
（= *Stop what you are doing. You might hurt someone.*）

11. *I don't mind if I do.* (6-8-15)

　　這句話是用在接受東西時的一種禮貌和幽默的說法，字
面的意思是「我不介意我這麼做。」引申為「那可太好了！」
【詳見「麥克米倫高級英漢雙解辭典」p.1263】

　　I don't mind if I do.
　　= That sounds great.
　　= It would be a pleasure.

12. *I don't buy it.* (8-16-30)

　　buy 最常見的意思是「買」，你願意買的東西，代表你
「相信」它的品質，所以 buy 在此引申為「相信」（= *believe*）
的意思。【詳見「麥克米倫高級英漢雙解辭典」p.264】

　　I don't buy it.
　　= Your excuse is not believable.
　　= I find that hard to believe.
　　　　excuse〔ɪk'skjus〕*n.* 藉口

13. *I had the time of my life*. (10-9-16)

這句話的字面的意思是「我有我生命的時間。」引申爲「享受生命。」就是「玩得很愉快。」

I had the time of my life.
= I had a good time.
= I enjoyed myself thoroughly.
= It was a blast.
= It was a memorable experience.

enjoy oneself 玩得愉快
thoroughly〔'θɝolɪ〕*adv.* 完全地
blast〔blæst〕*n.* 愉快的經歷
memorable〔'mɛmərəbl̩〕*adj.* 難忘的

14. *Can it wait?* (11-11-23)

這句話的意思是「這件事情可以等一下嗎?」用來表示目前還忙不過來,無法馬上處理。

Can it wait?
= Is it urgent?
= Can you come back at another time?

urgent〔'ɝdʒənt〕*adj.* 緊急的;迫切的

15. *They murdered us*. (11-13-25)

Murder 的主要意思是「謀殺」,引申爲「徹底擊敗」(= *defeat someone completely*) 的意思,例如:We were murdered by the last year's champions. (我們慘敗給去年的冠軍。)【champion〔'tʃæmpɪən〕*n.* 冠軍】

16. *Monday works better for me*. (12-9-18)

這句話字面的意思是「對我來說週一比較行得通。」意思就是「對我來說週一比較方便。」也可說成:Monday is more convenient for me.